Coloring A Course in Miracles Vol. 6:

Mantra Mandalas Coloring Pages™

By
Kristin G. Hatch &
Delaina J. Miller

Published by Content X Design Inc.
P.O. Box 8754
Kansas City, MO. 64114

www.contentxdesign.com

ISBN-10: 1-942005-19-9
ISBN-13: 978-1-942005-19-3

To learn more about the series visit:
ColoringACIM.com

Enjoy this book:

Grab crayons or colored pencils,
find a nice place to relax,
turn on your favorite music
take a deep breath
& have fun!

Let the lessons from the workbook of *A Course in Miracles* seep into your mind as you color each Mantra Mandala. Allow the power of the words to become a part of your day.

Coloring A Course in Miracles Vol. 6: Mantra Mandalas Coloring Pages™, is a coloring book inspired by the famous and popular spiritual transformation study — *A Course in Miracles* by Helen Schucman & William Thetford. Volume six covers lessons 301-365 of the workbook, giving you 64 mandalas to color.

Coloring A Course in Miracles allows students to meditate on each of the lessons for an extended period of time to evoke a deeper connection with the text.

A Mantra Mandala was created by pondering each ACIM lesson and choosing a word or words to create a mandala.

This meditative coloring practice is not only relaxing, it enables users to engage and absorb the lessons in a fun way.

Grab your crayons or colored pencils and dive in!

Workbook Lesson 301

And God Himself shall *wipe away* all tears.

Wipe Away

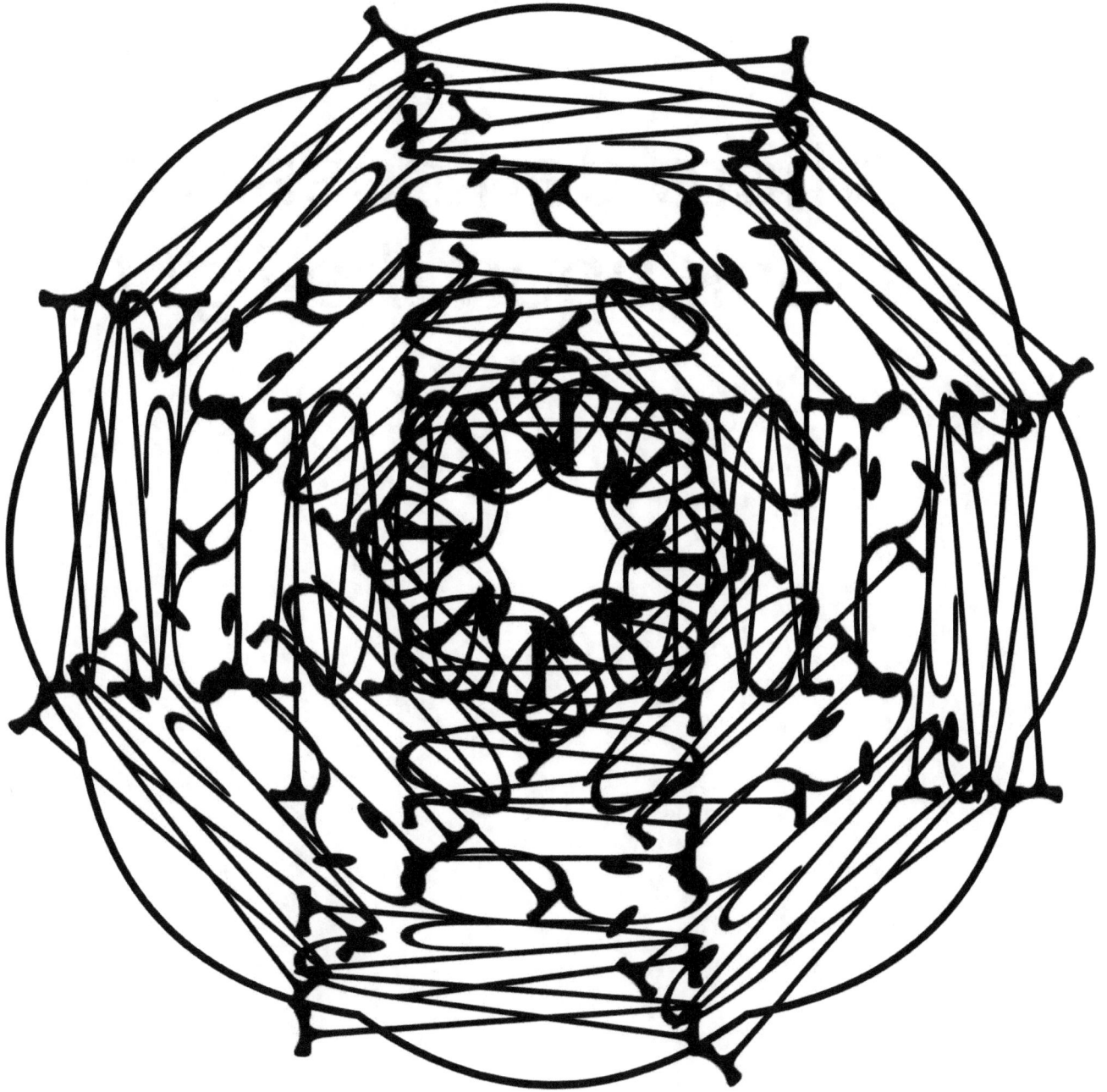

Workbook Lesson 302

Where darkness was I look upon *the light*.

The Light

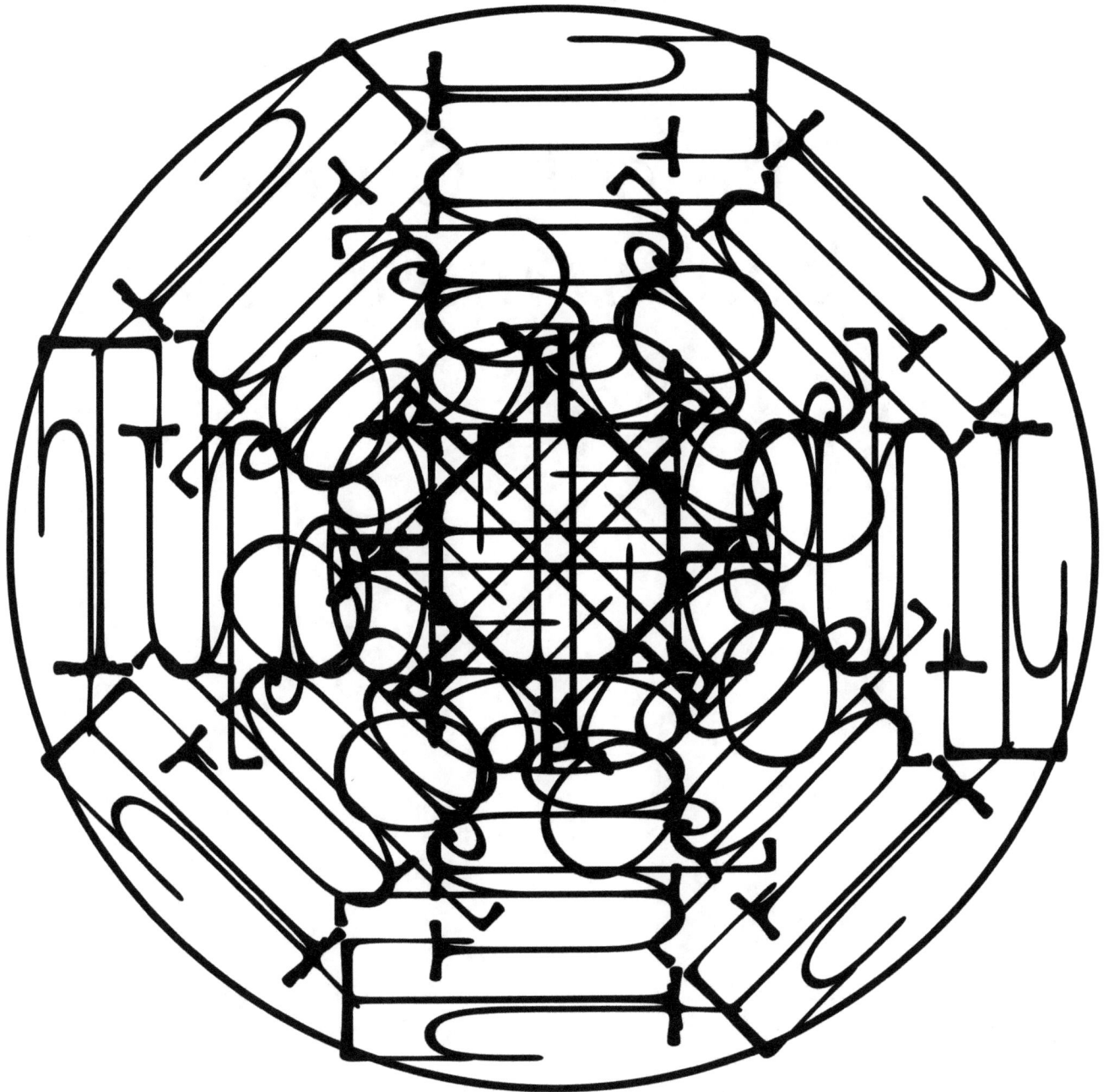

Workbook Lesson 303

The holy Christ is born *in me today*.

In Me Today

Workbook Lesson 304

Let not *my world* obscure the sight of Christ.

My World

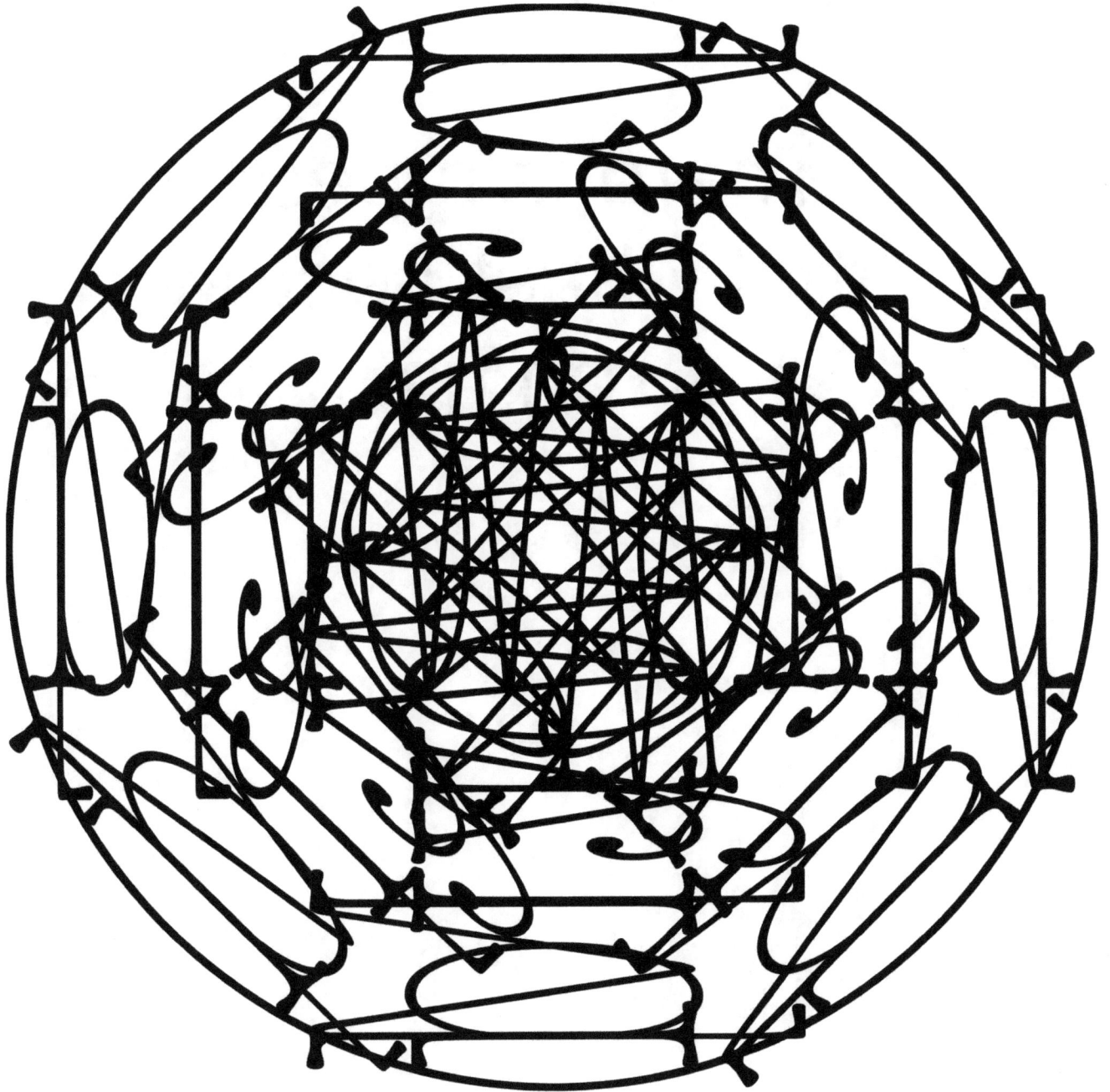

Workbook Lesson 305

There is a peace that Christ *bestows* on us.

Bestows

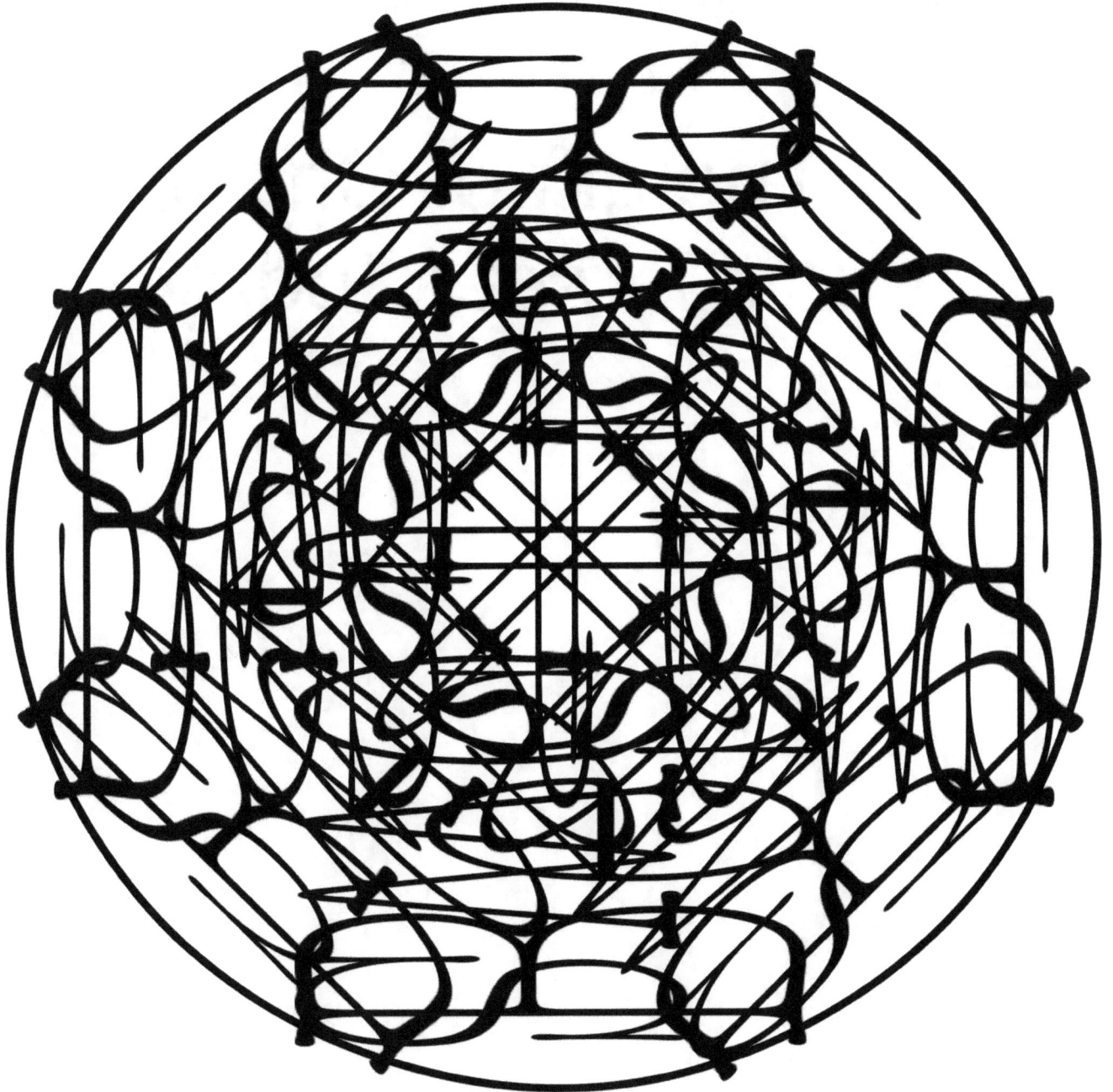

Workbook Lesson 306

The gift of Christ is *all I seek* today.

All I Seek

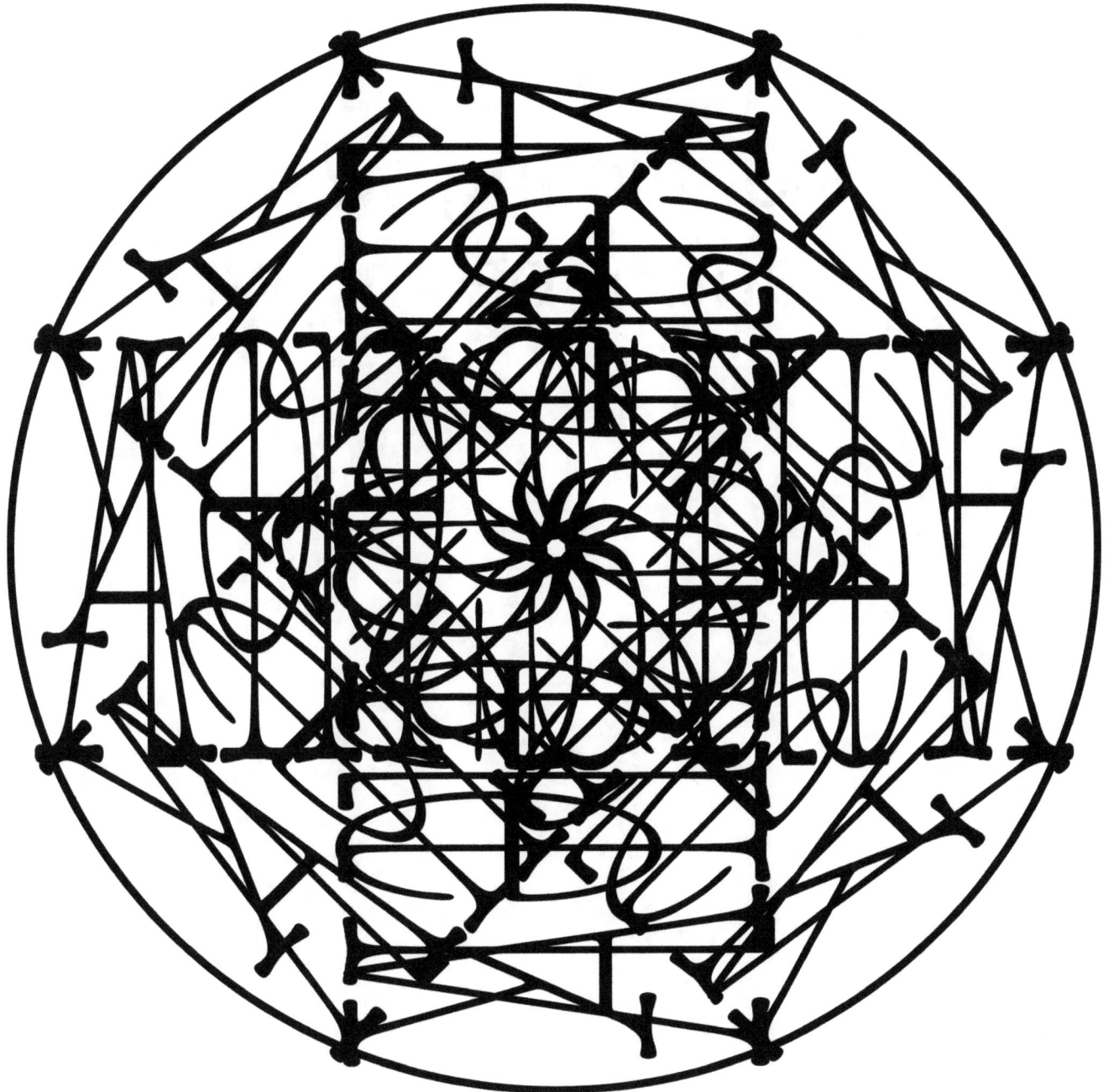

Workbook Lesson 307

Conflicting *wishes* cannot be my will.

Wishes

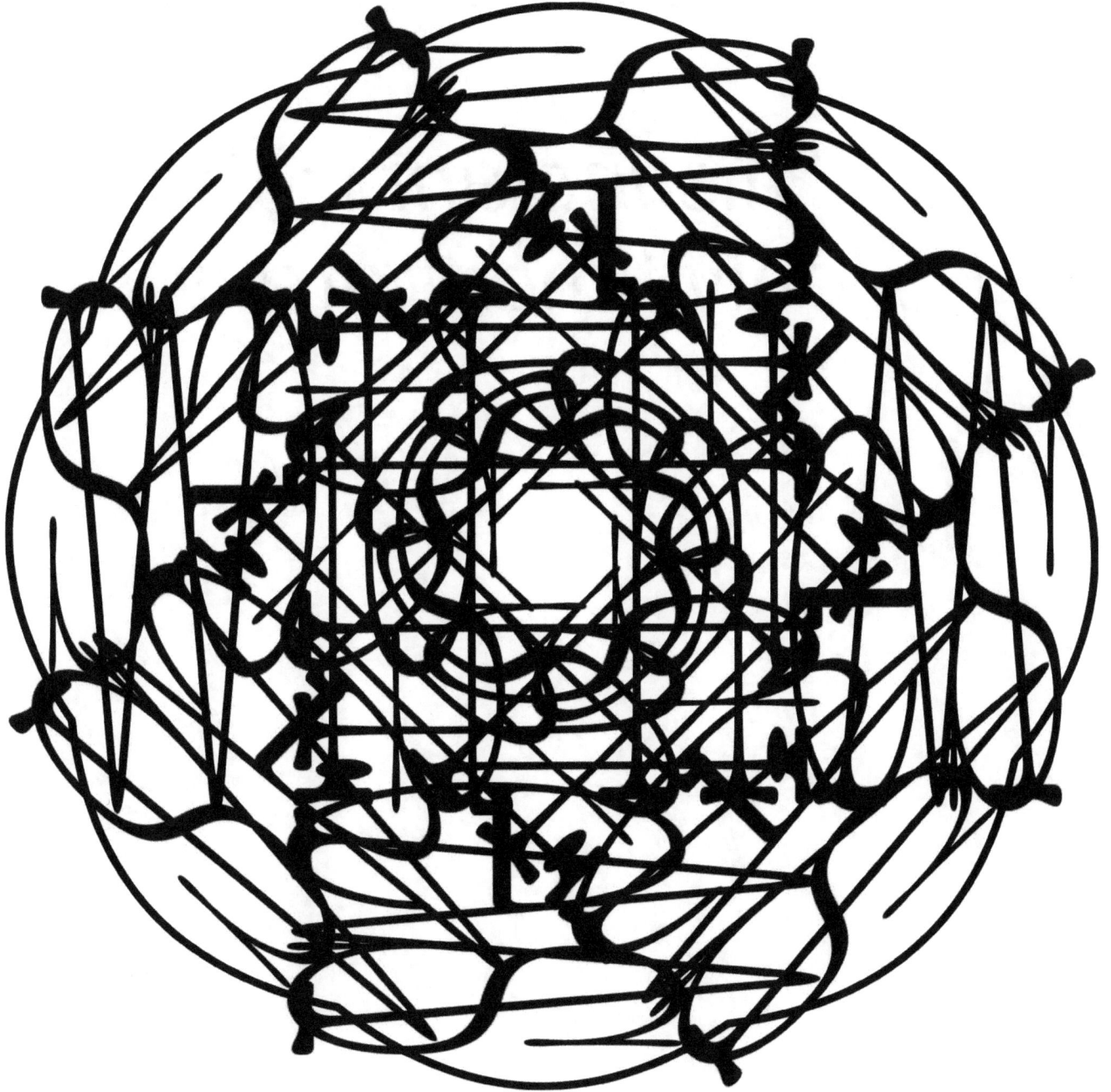

Workbook Lesson 308

This *instant* is the
only time there is.

Instant

Workbook Lesson 309

I will not fear to *look within* today.

Look Within

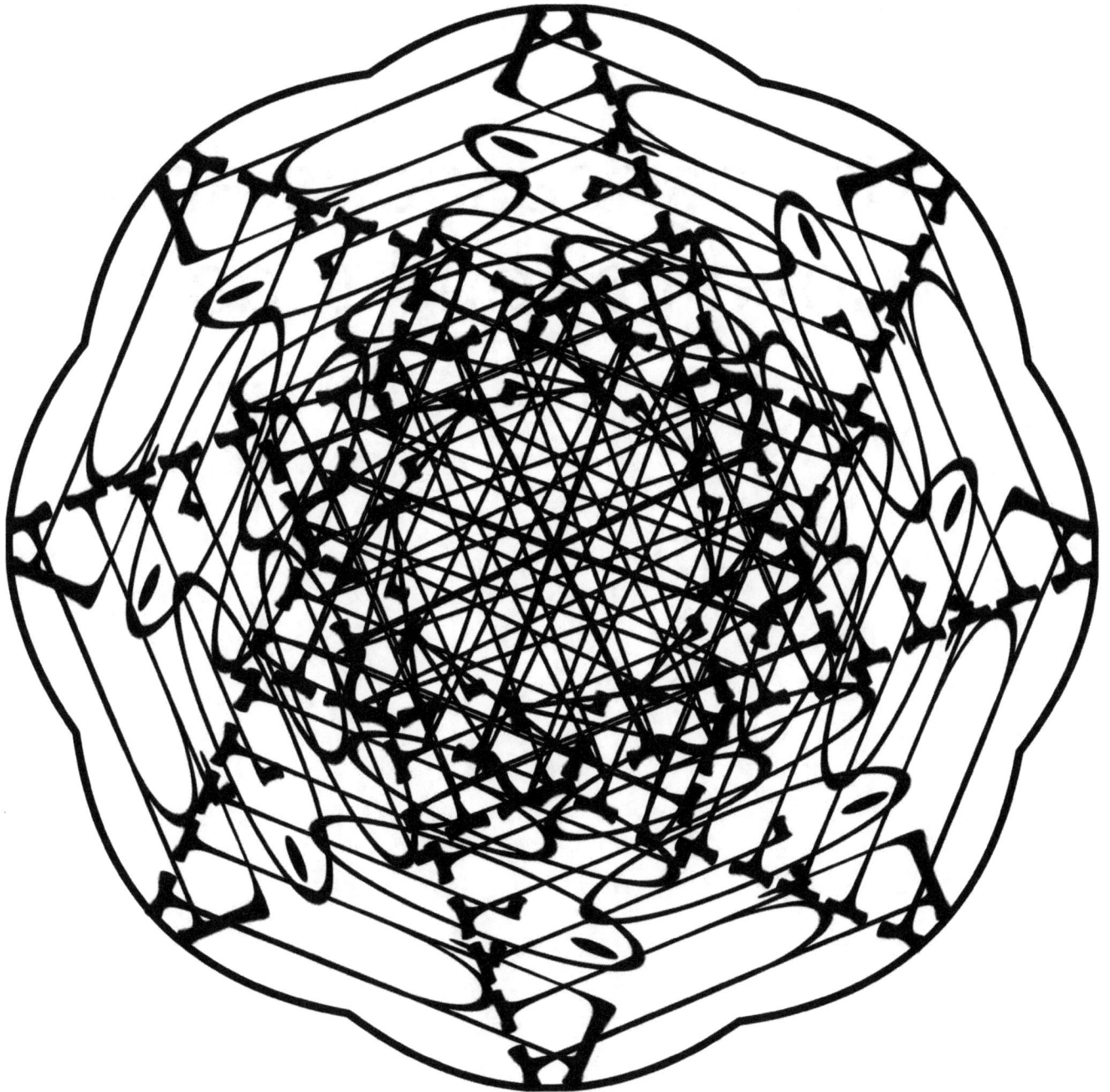

Workbook Lesson 310

In *fearlessness* and love I spend today.

Fearlessness

Workbook Lesson 311

I judge *all things*
as I would
have them be.

All Things

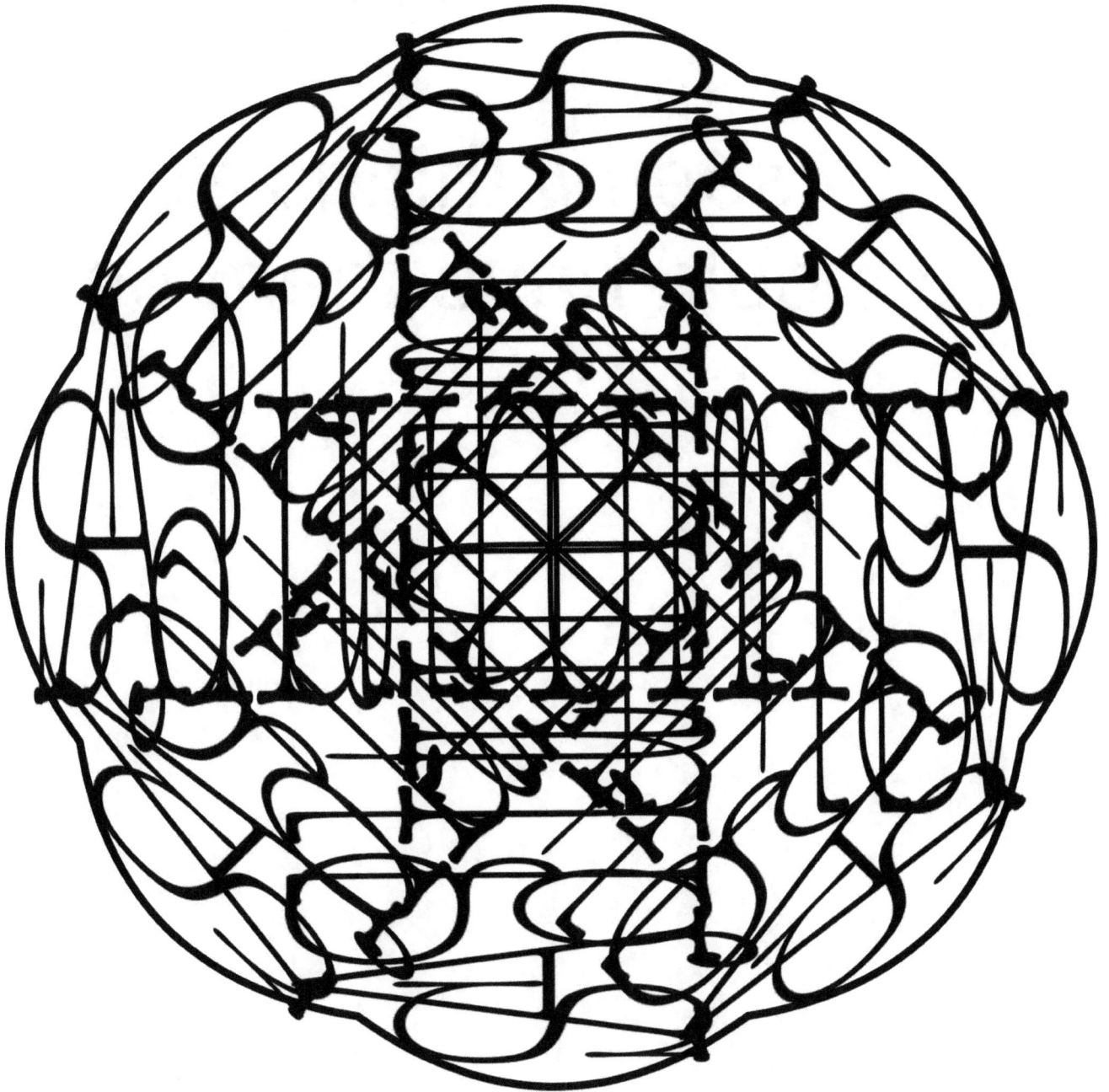

Workbook Lesson 312

I see all things as I would have them be.

I See All

Workbook Lesson 313

Now let a new *perception* come to me.

Perception

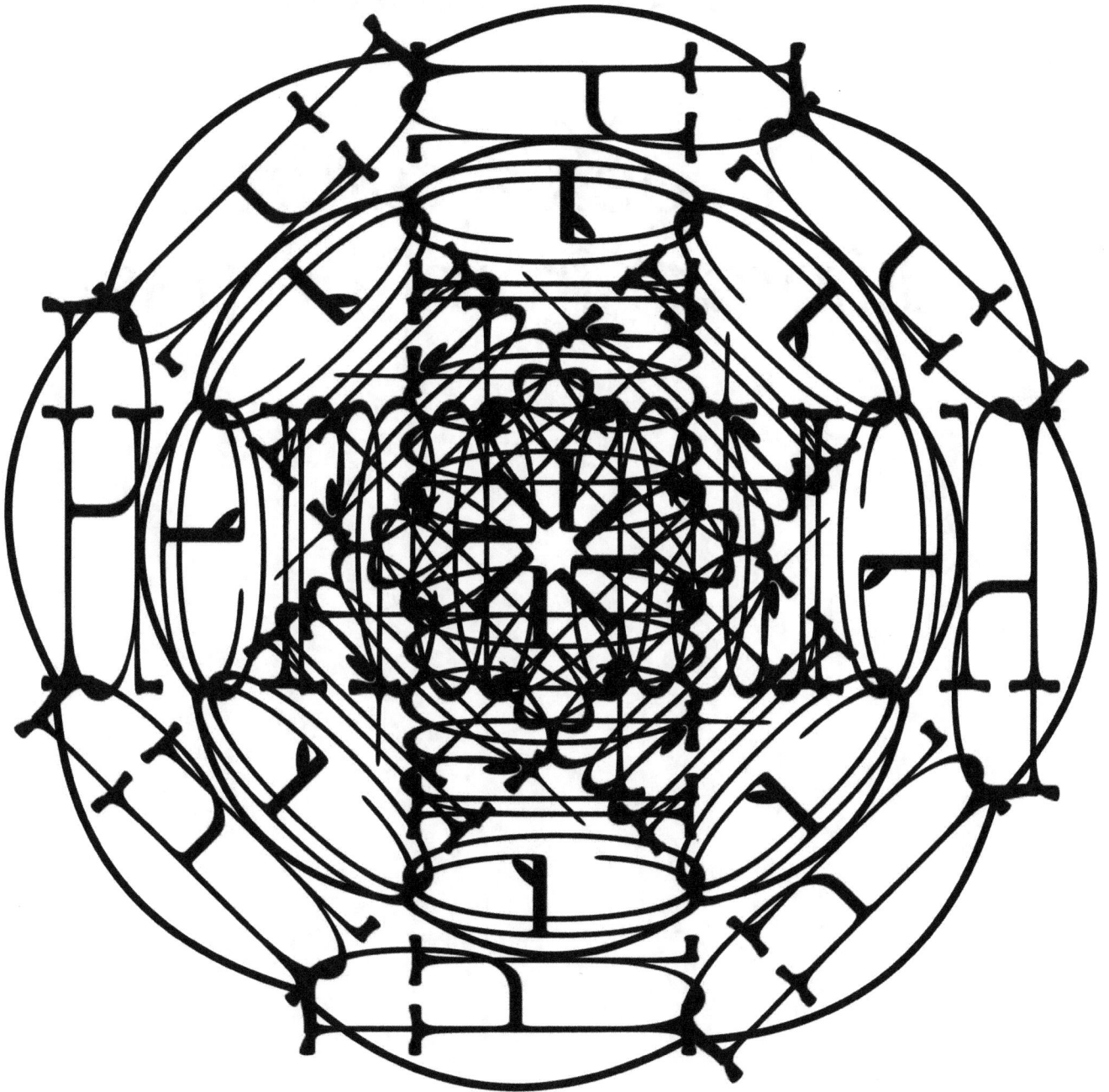

Workbook Lesson 314

I seek a *future*
different from the past.

Future

Workbook Lesson 315

All gifts my brothers give *belong* to me.

Belong

Workbook Lesson 316

All gifts I give my brothers are my own.

All Gifts

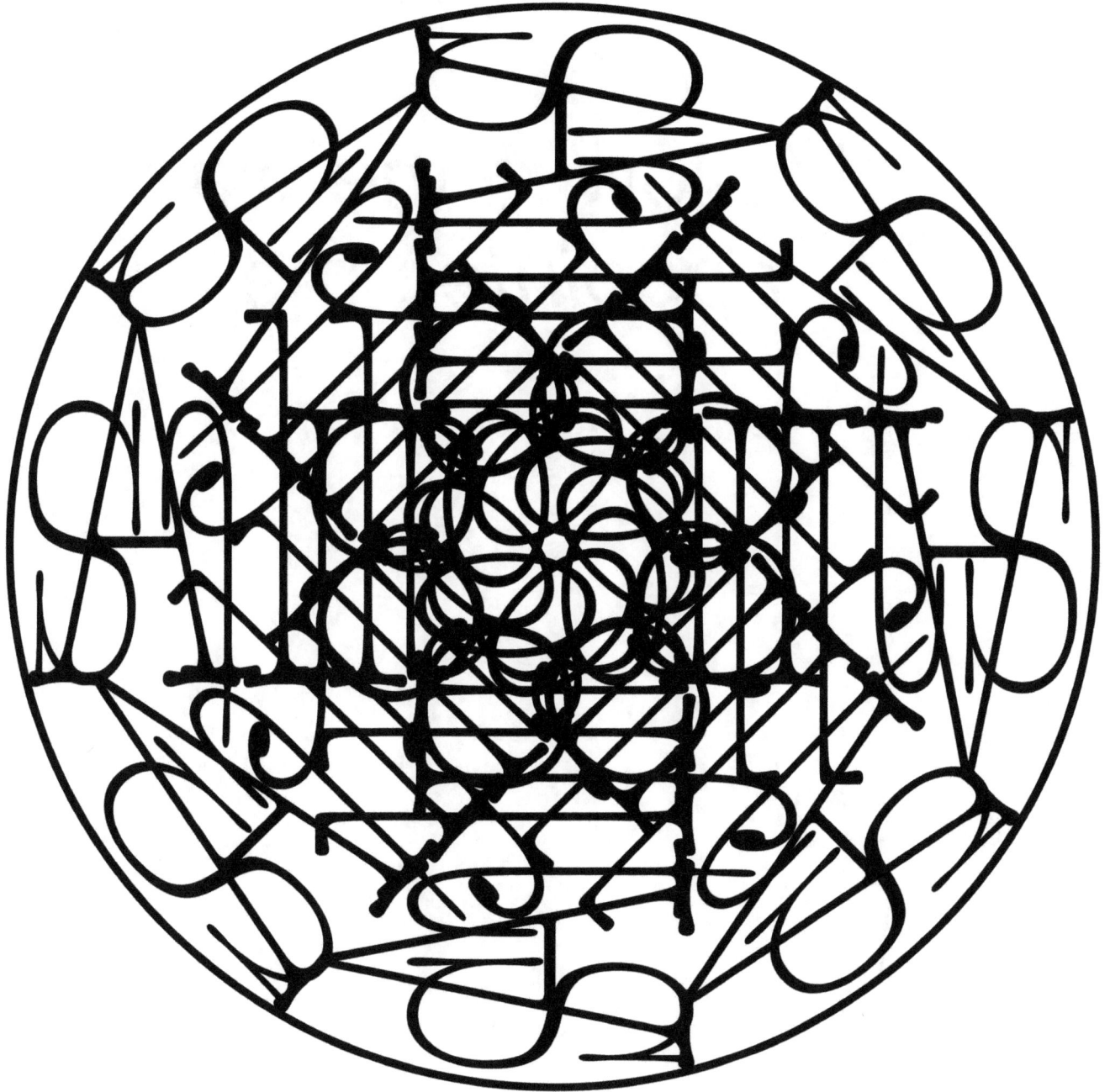

Workbook Lesson 317

I follow in the way *appointed* me.

Appointed

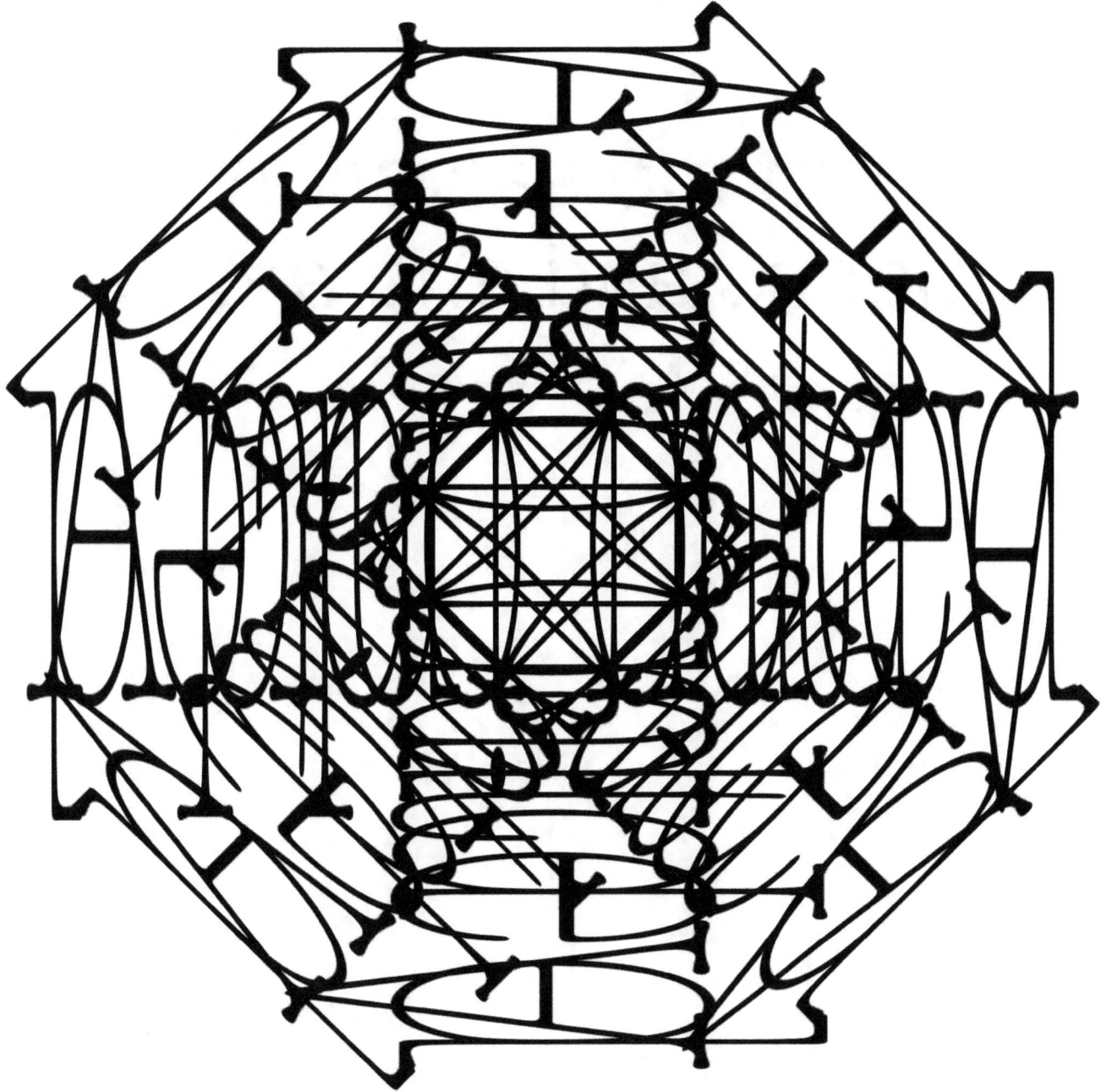

Workbook Lesson 318

In me salvation's
means and end *are one*.

Are One

Workbook Lesson 319

I came for the *salvation*
of the world.

Salvation

Workbook Lesson 320

My Father gives
all power unto me.

All Power

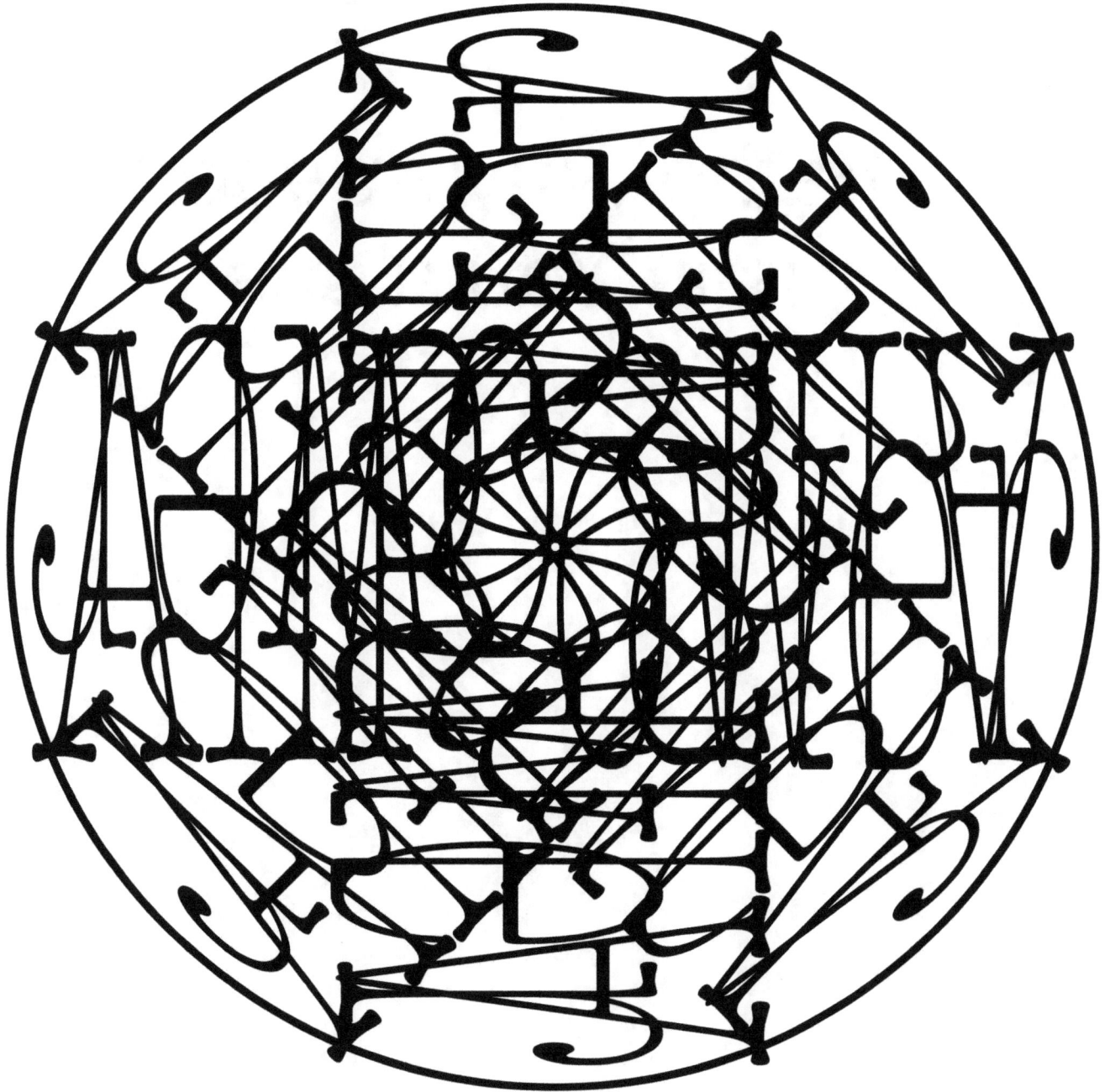

Workbook Lesson 321

Father, my *freedom* is in You alone.

Freedom

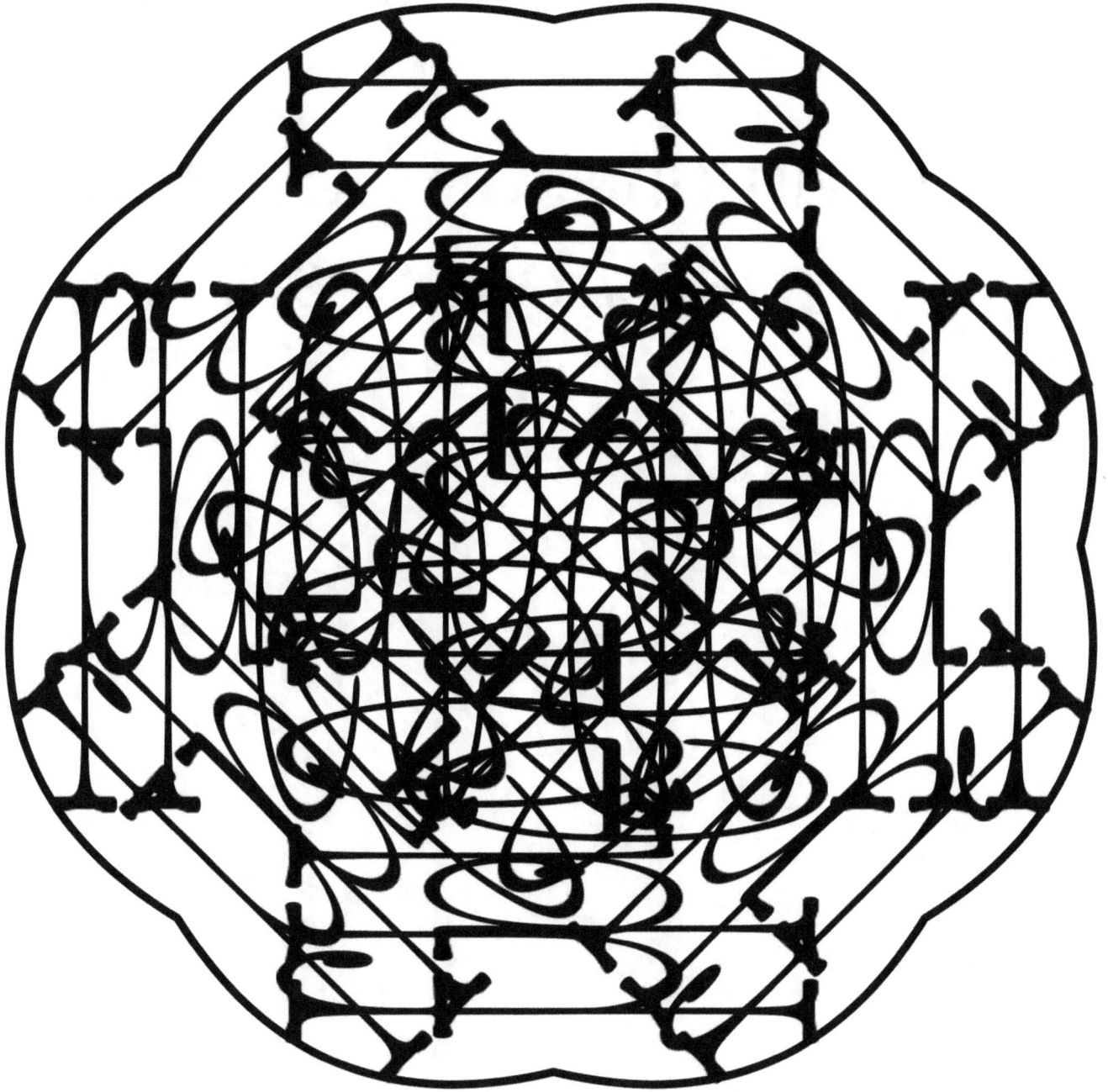

Workbook Lesson 322

I can give up but what was *never real*.

Never Real

Workbook Lesson 323

I *gladly* make the "sacrifice" of fear.

Gladly

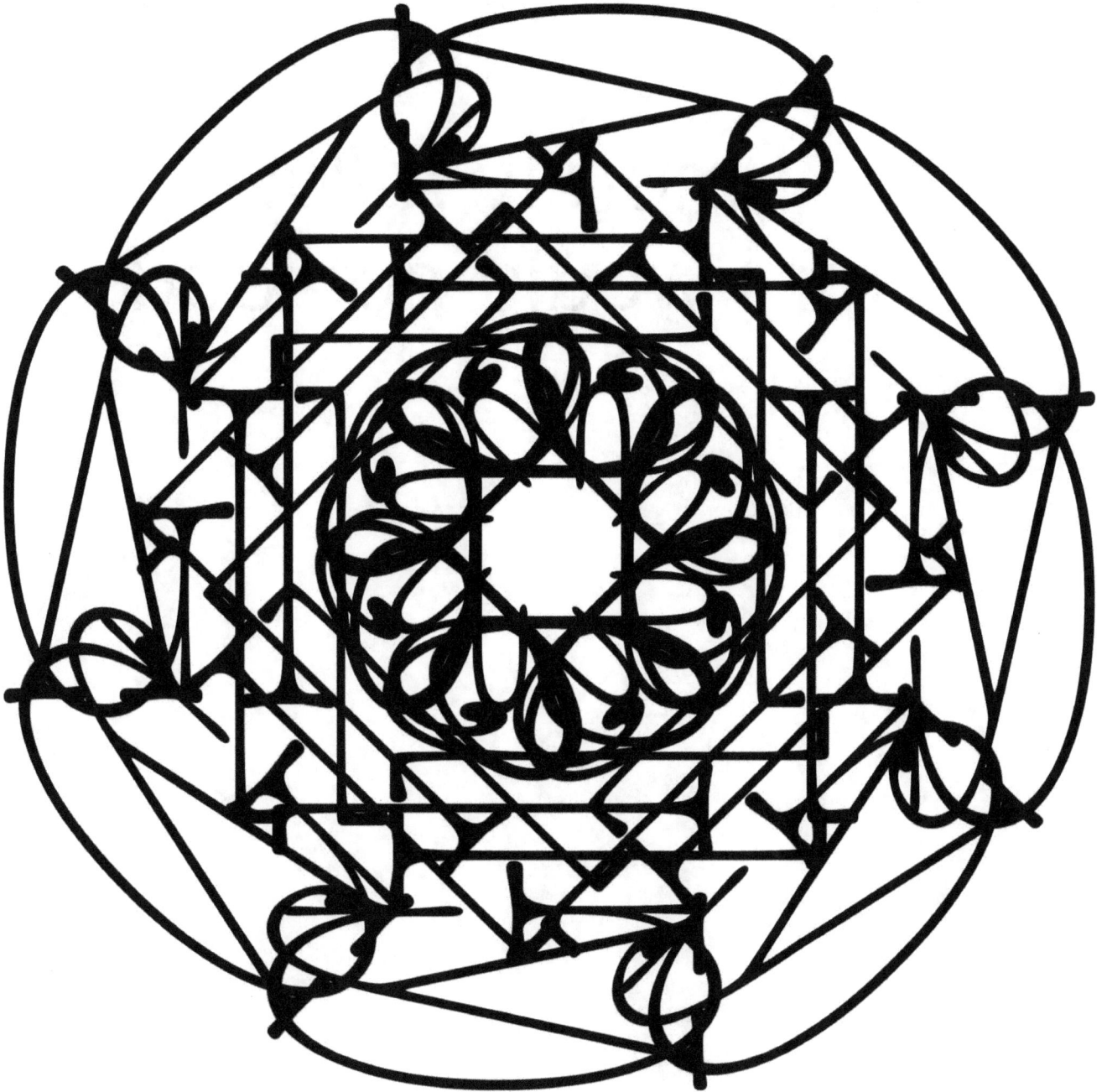

Workbook Lesson 324

I merely *follow*,
for I would not lead.

Follow

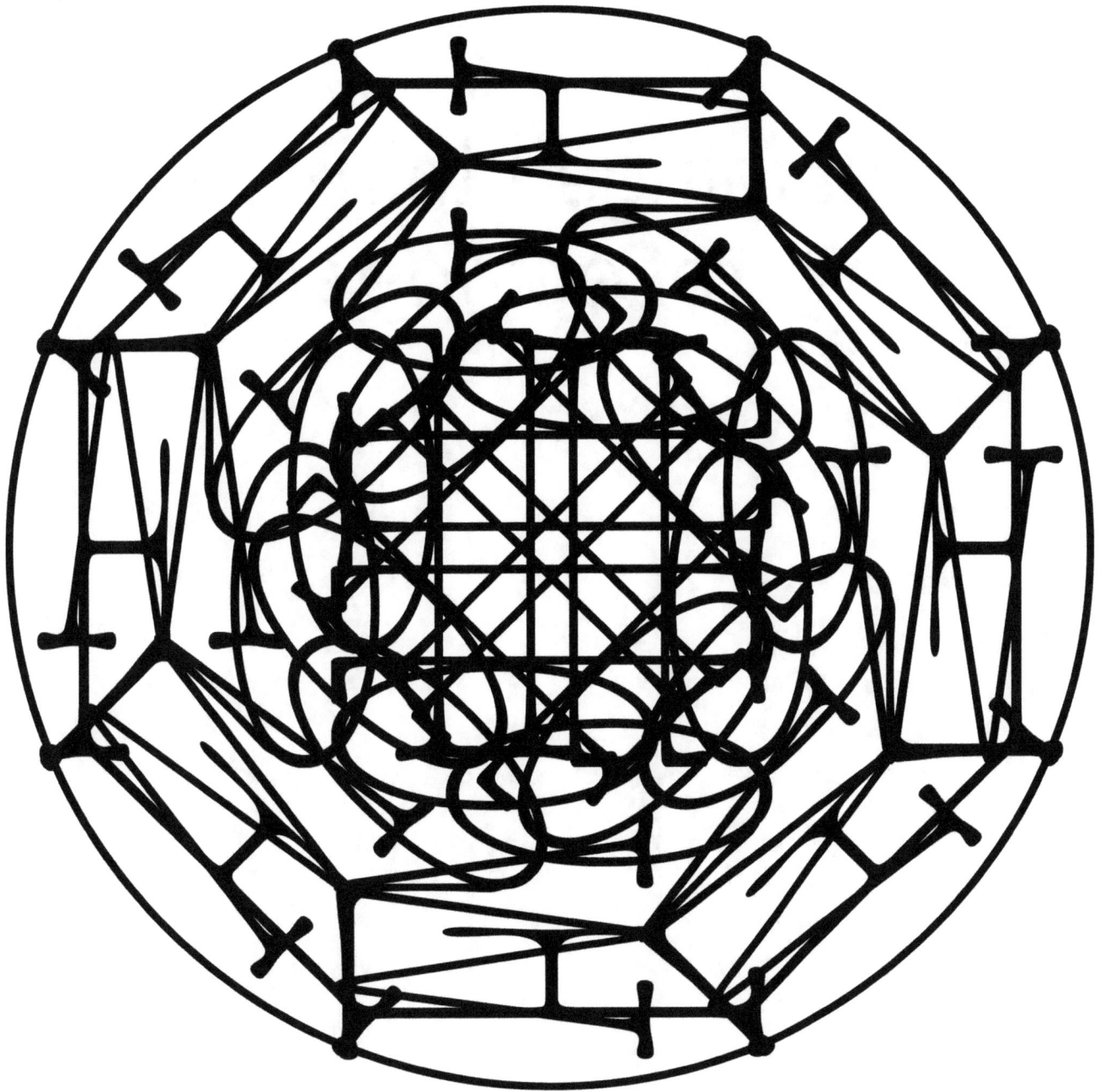

Workbook Lesson 325

All things I think I see reflect *ideas*.

Ideas

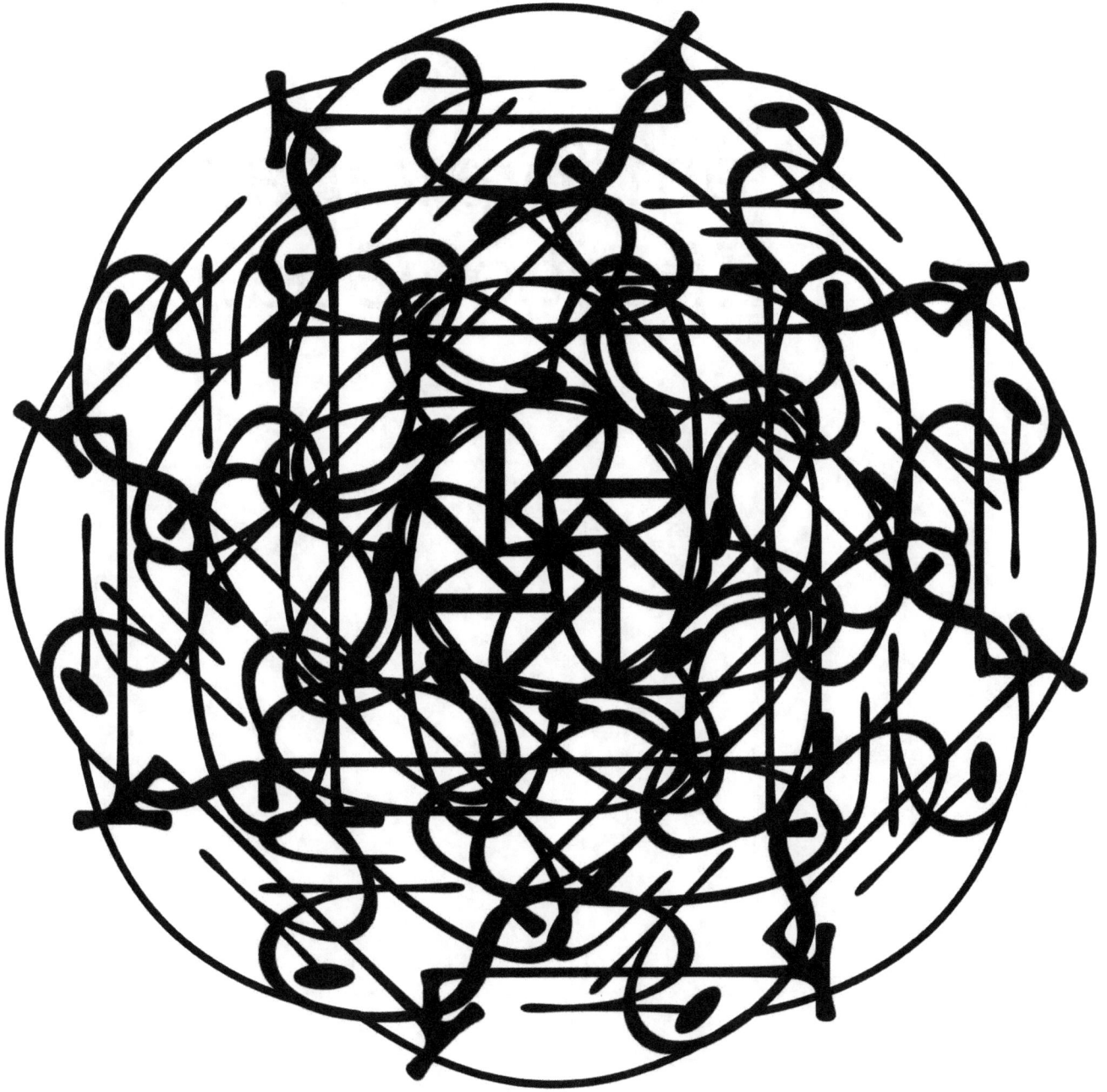

Workbook Lesson 326

I am *forever* an Effect of God.

Forever

Workbook Lesson 327

I need but call and
You will *answer* me.

Answer

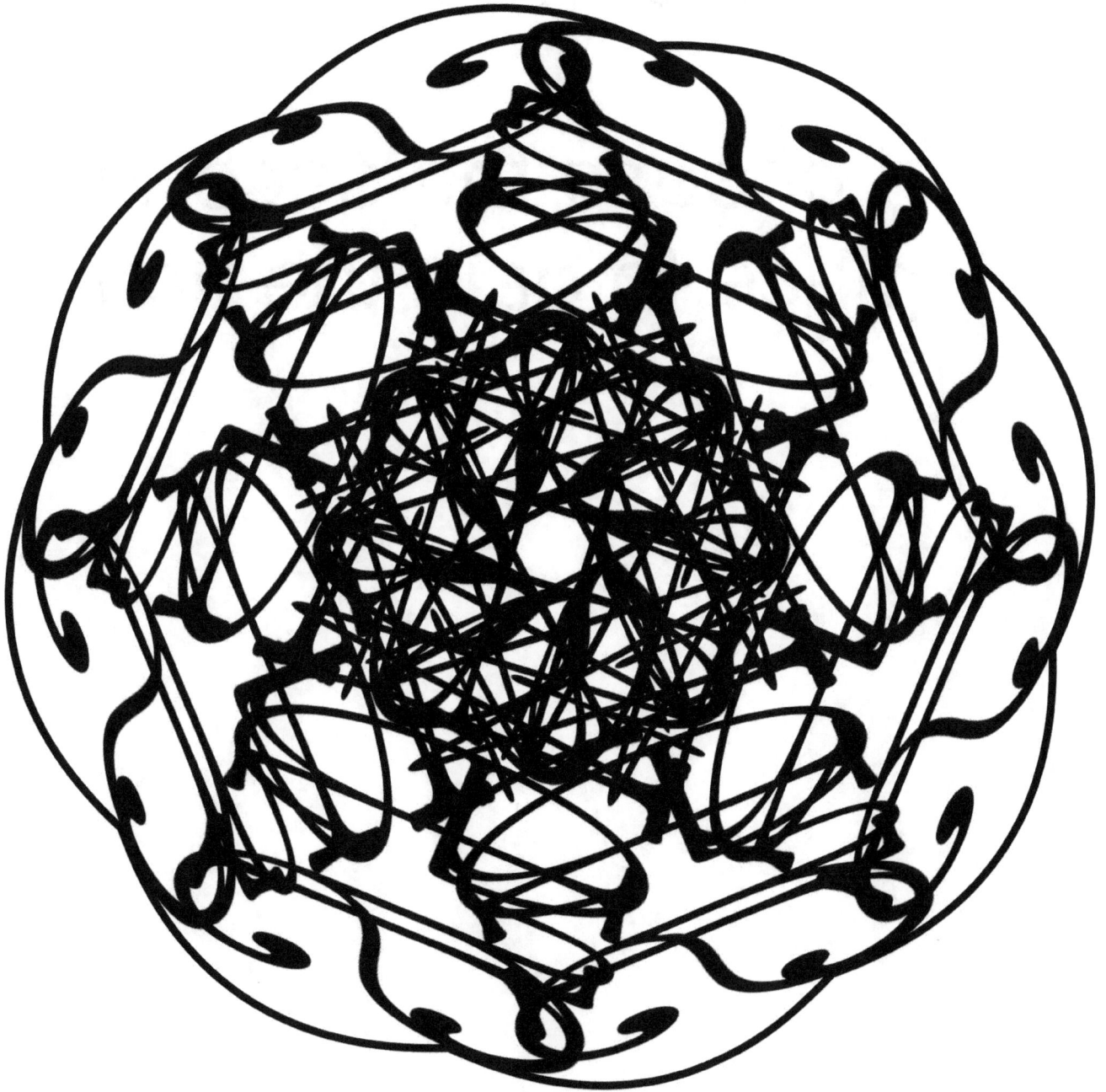

Workbook Lesson 328

I *choose* the second place to gain the first.

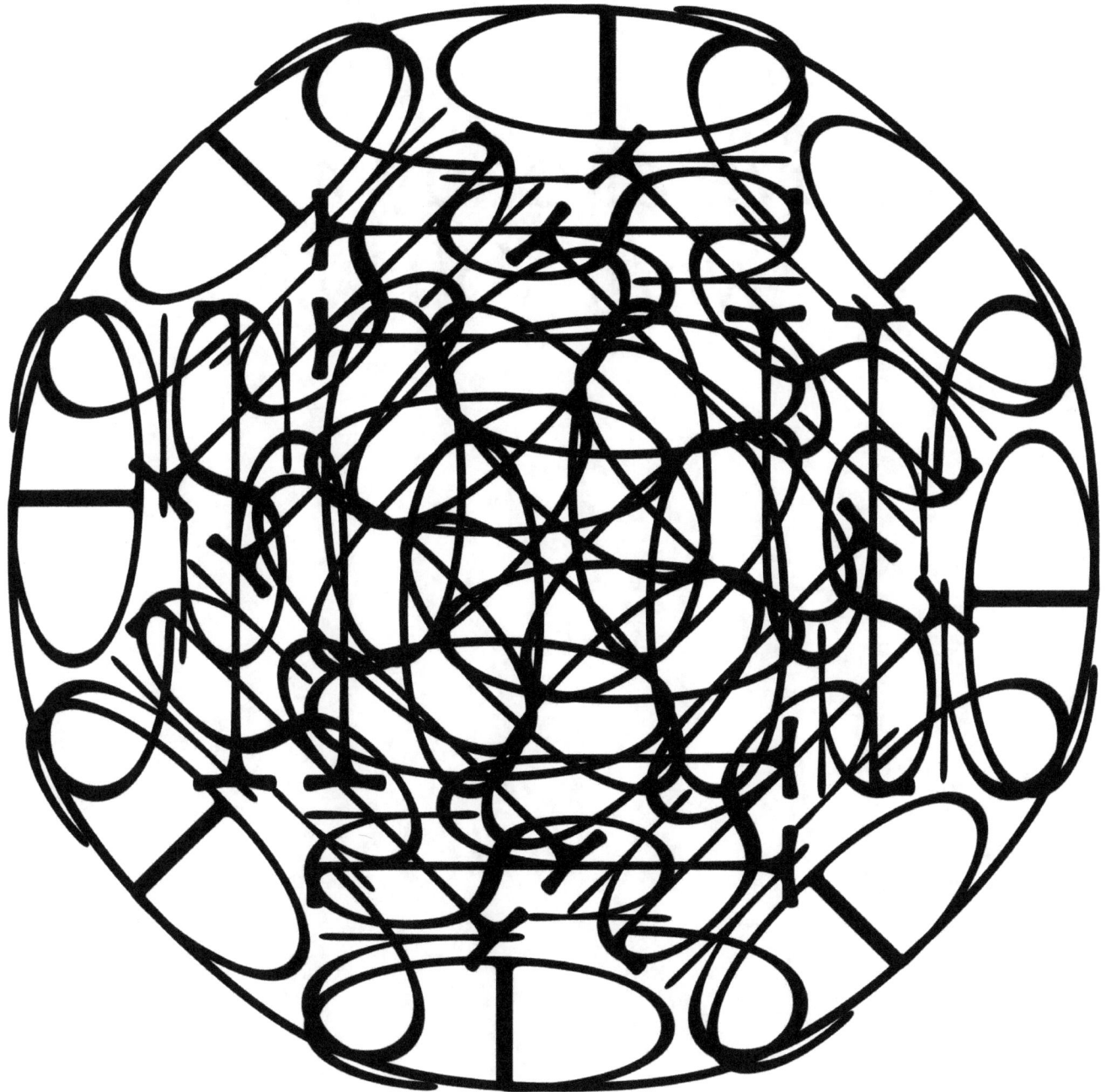

Choose

Workbook Lesson 329

I have already *chosen*
what You will.

Chosen

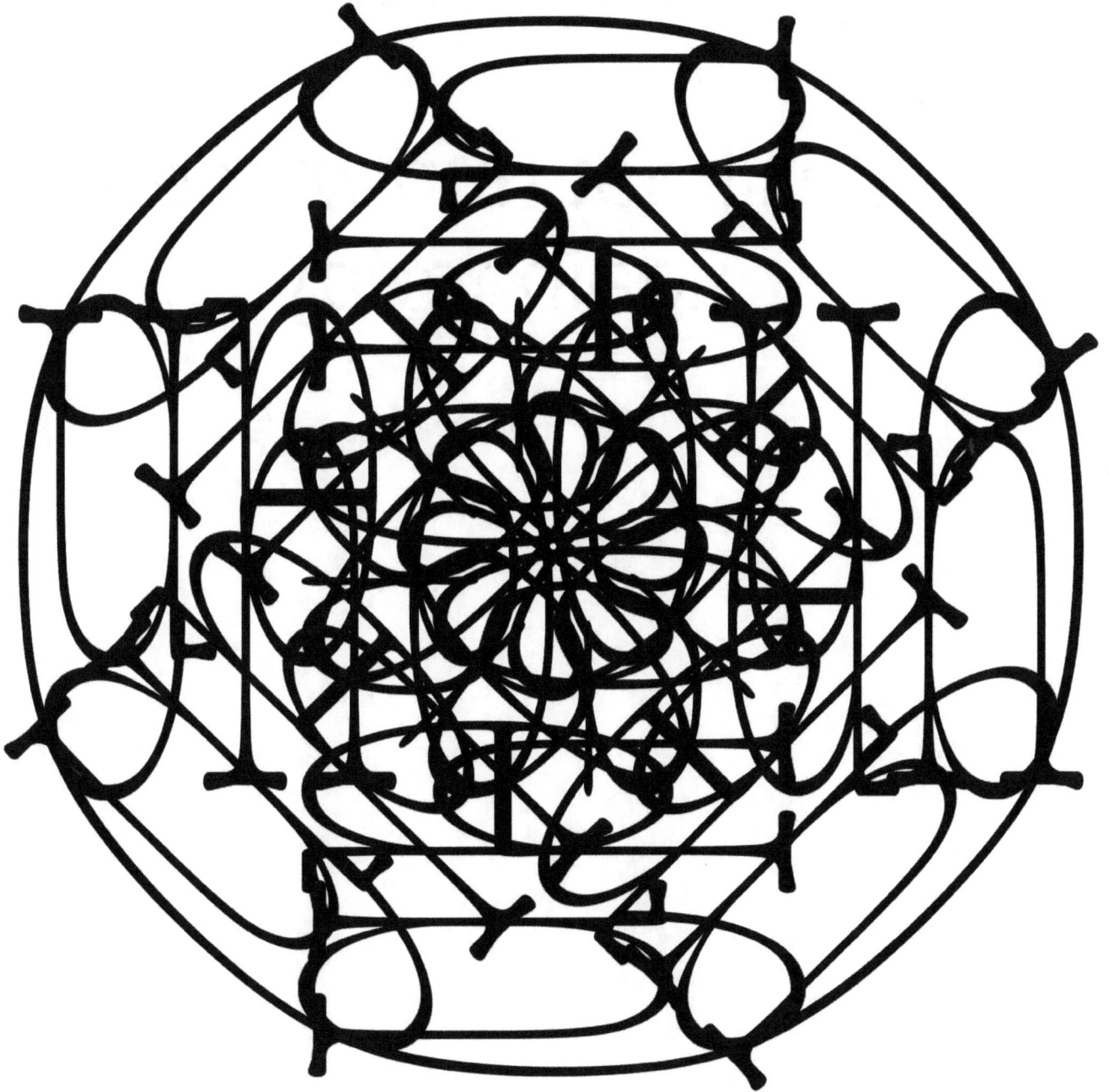

Workbook Lesson 330

I will not hurt *myself* again today.

Myself

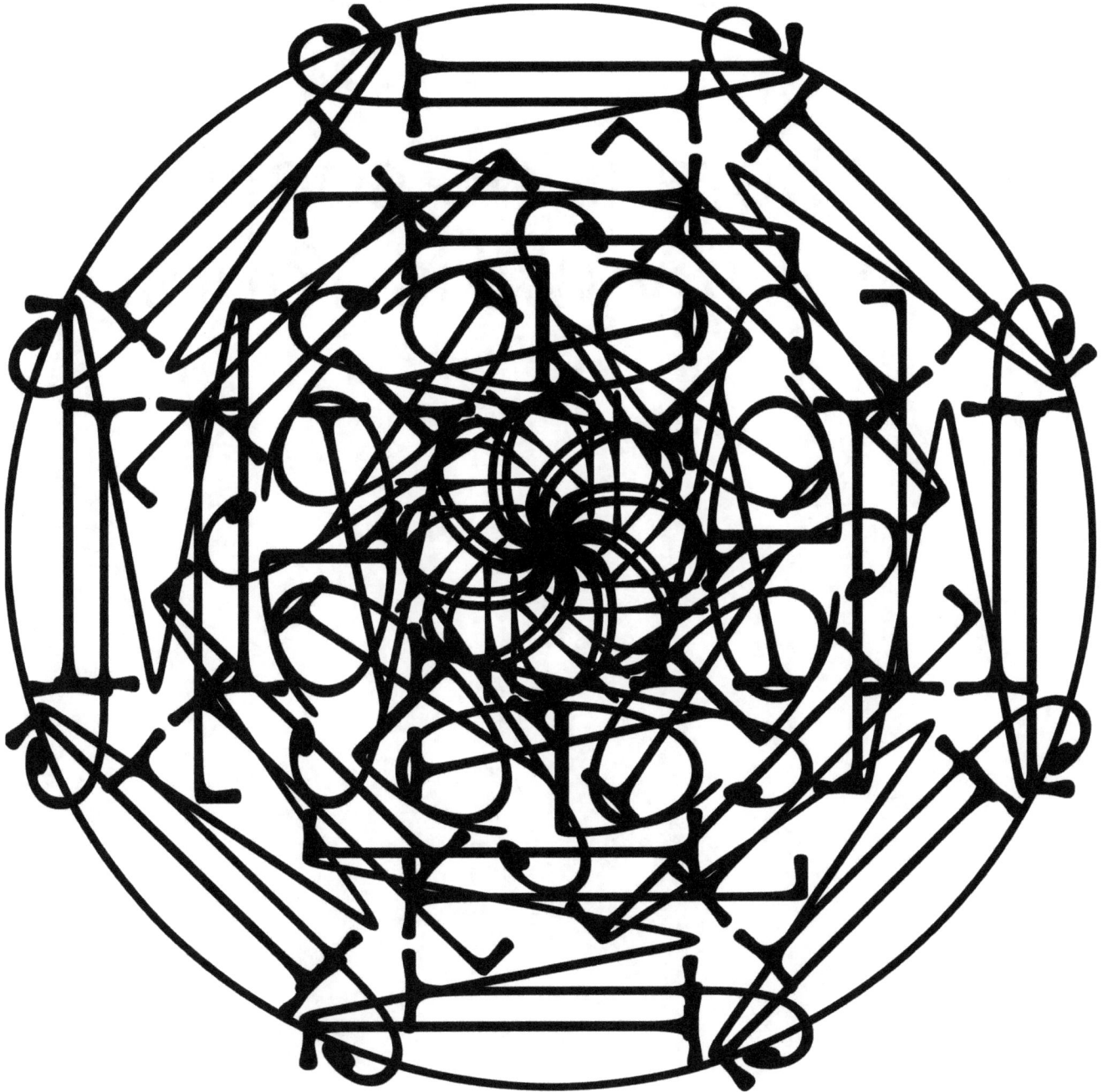

Workbook Lesson 331

There is no conflict,
for *my will* is Yours.

My Will

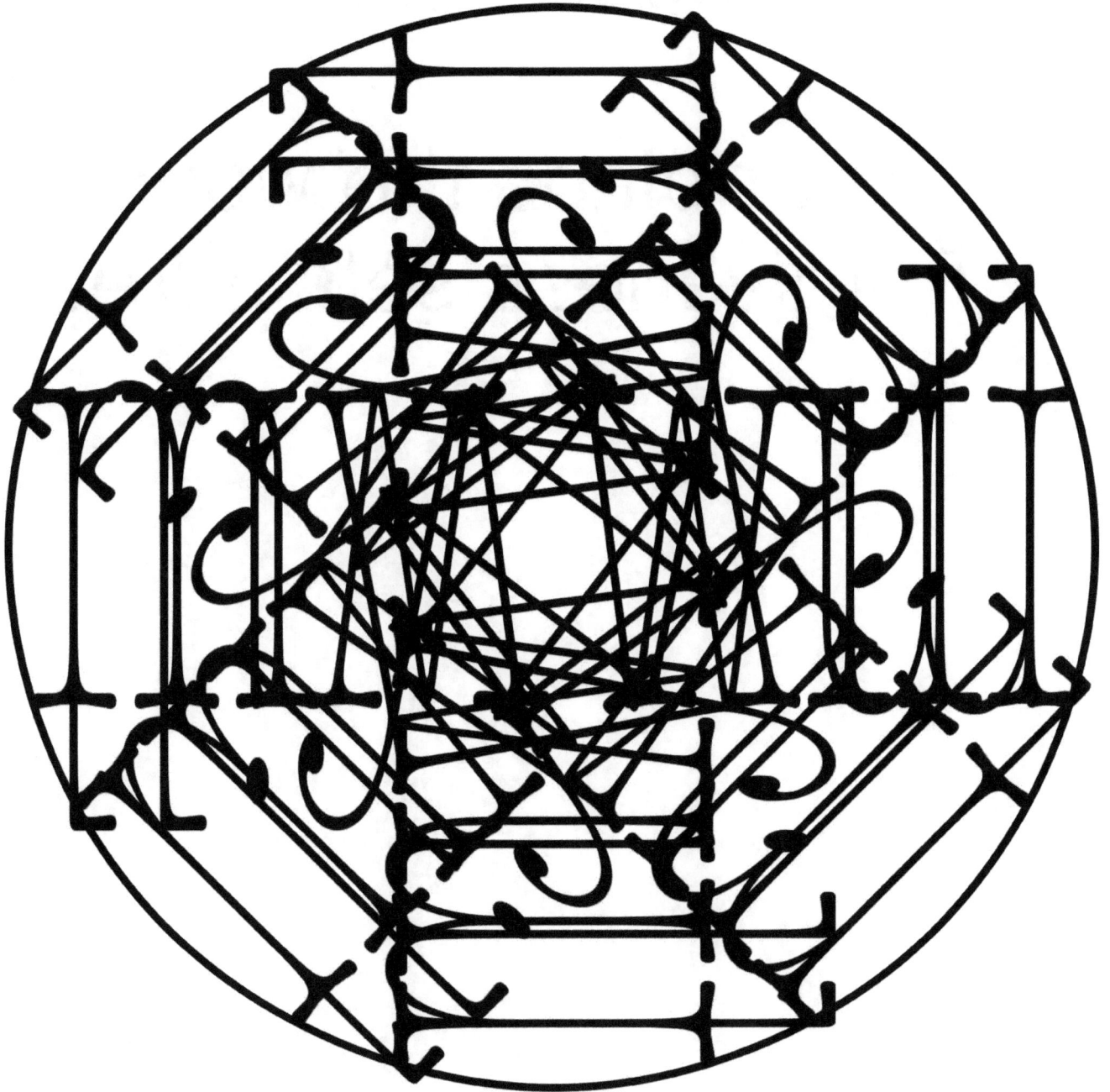

Workbook Lesson 332

Fear binds the world.
Forgiveness sets *it free*.

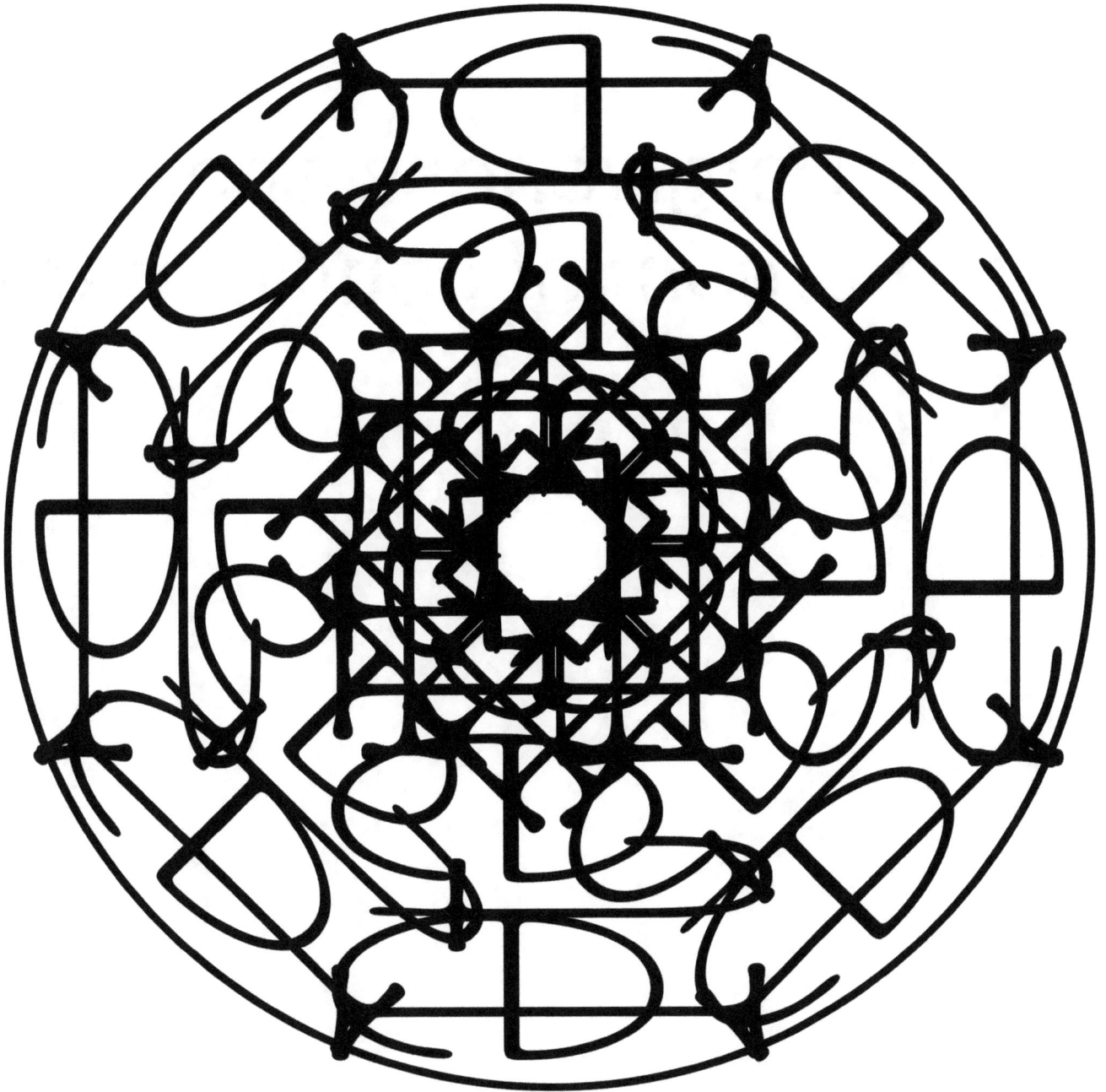

It Free

Workbook Lesson 333

Forgiveness ends
the *dream* of conflict here.

Dream

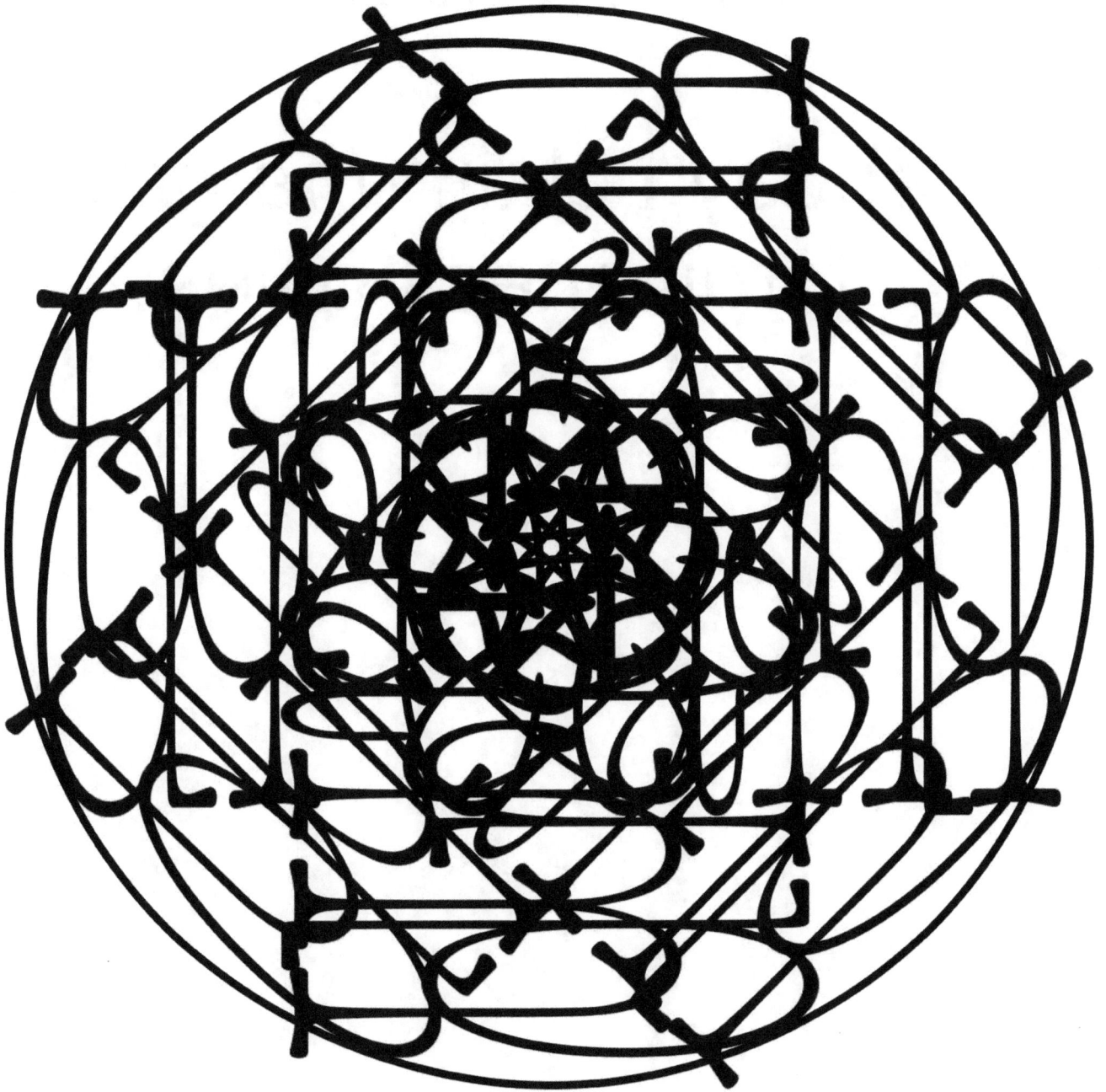

Workbook Lesson 334

Today I claim *the gifts* forgiveness gives.

The Gifts

Workbook Lesson 335

I choose *to see* my brother's sinlessness.

To See

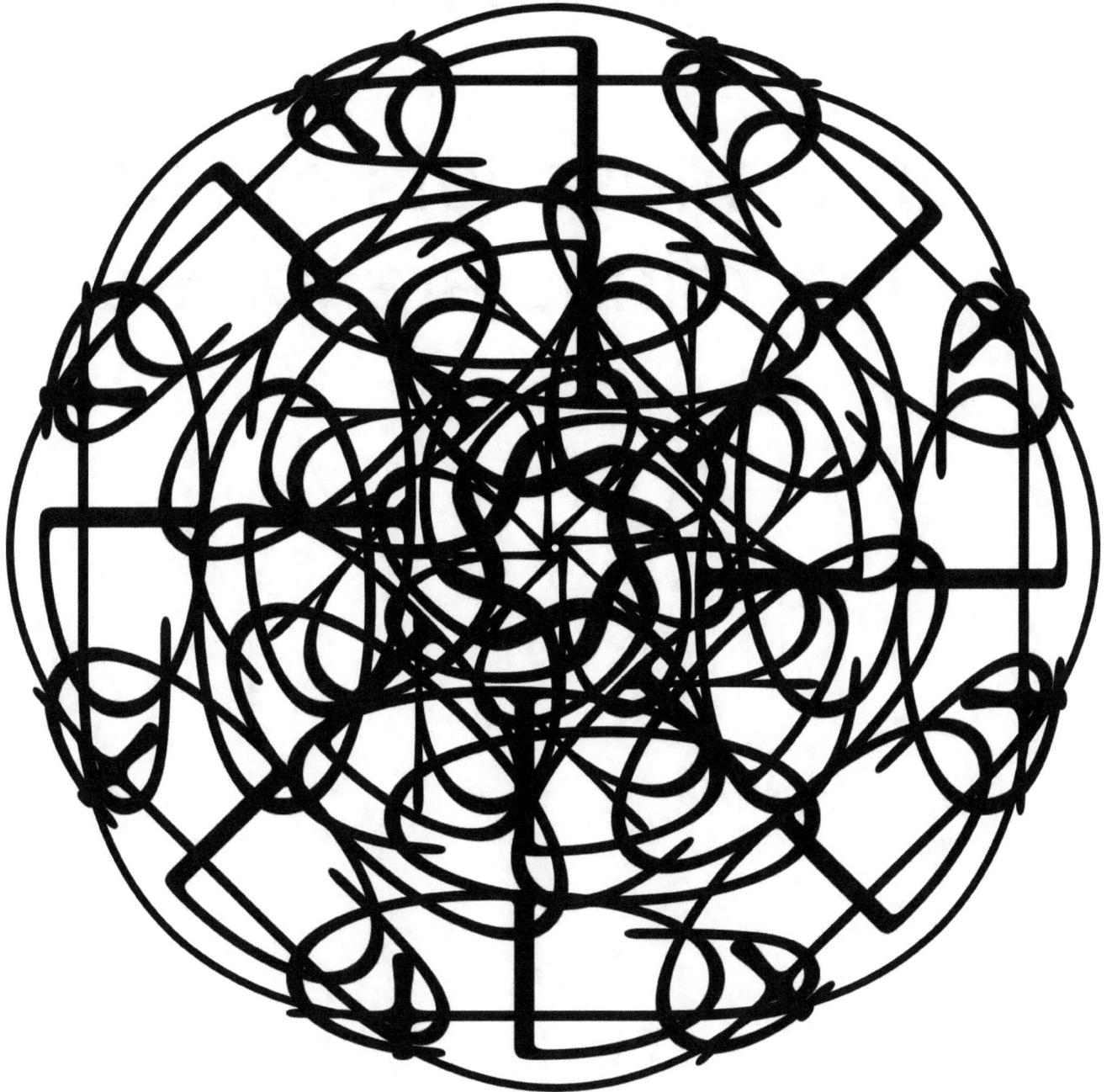

Workbook Lesson 336

Forgiveness lets me know that minds are *joined*.

Joined

Workbook Lesson 337

My sinlessness *protects* me from all harm.

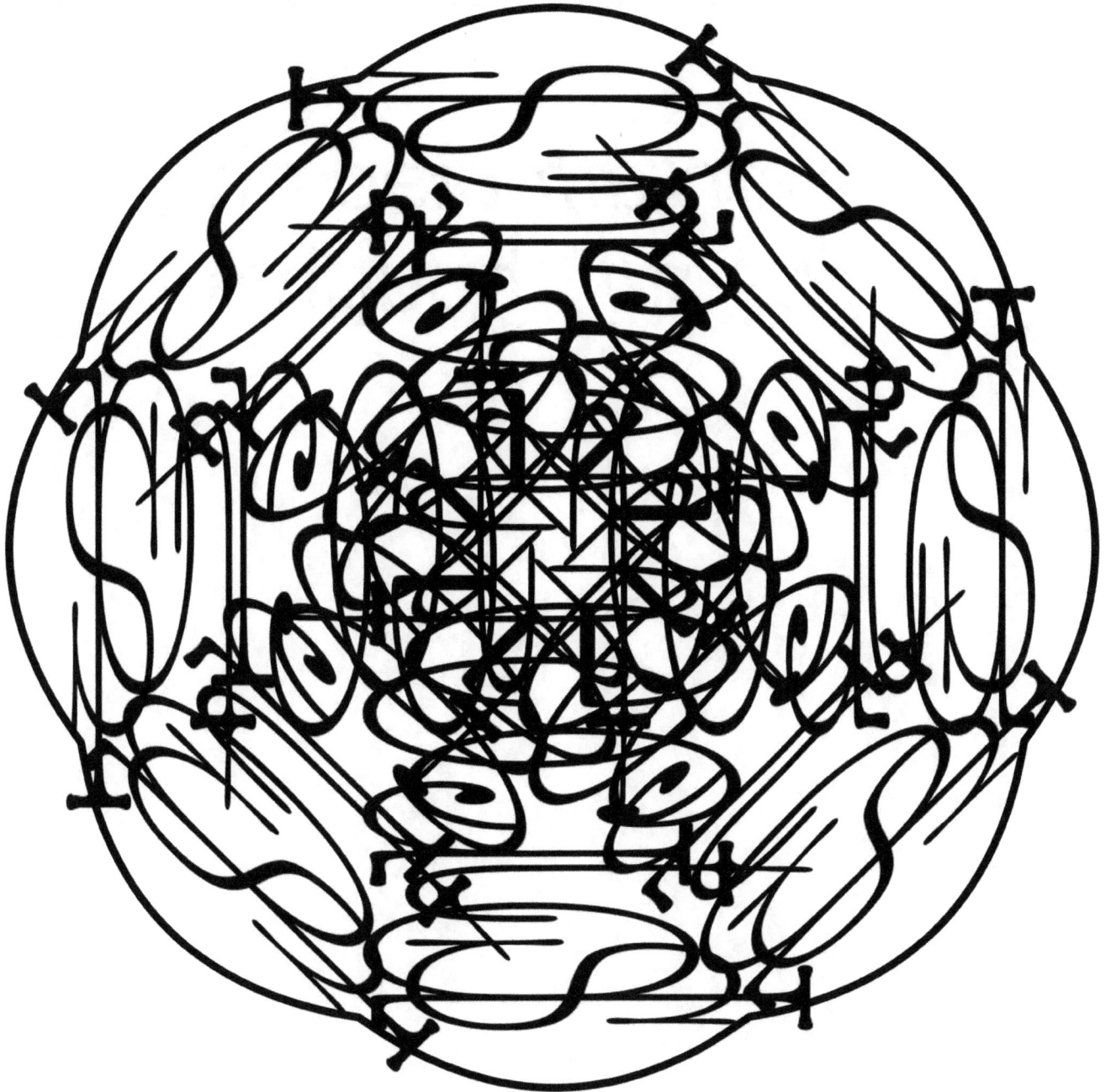

Protects

Workbook Lesson 338

I am *affected* only by my thoughts.

Affected

Workbook Lesson 339

I will receive whatever I *request*.

Request

Workbook Lesson 340

I can *be free* of suffering today.

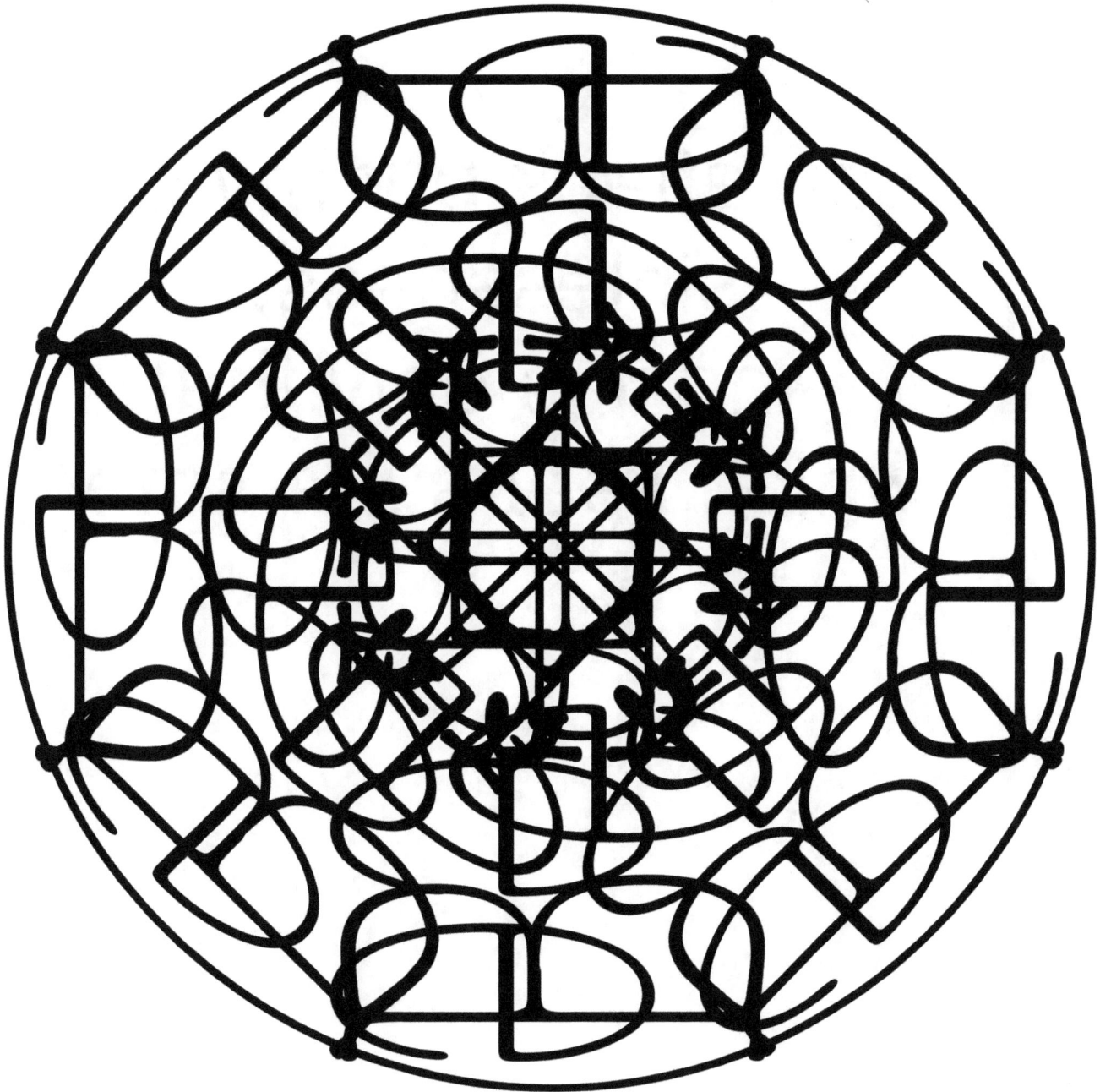

Be Free

Workbook Lesson 341

I can attack but my own
sinlessness,
And it is only that
which *keeps me* safe.

Keeps Me

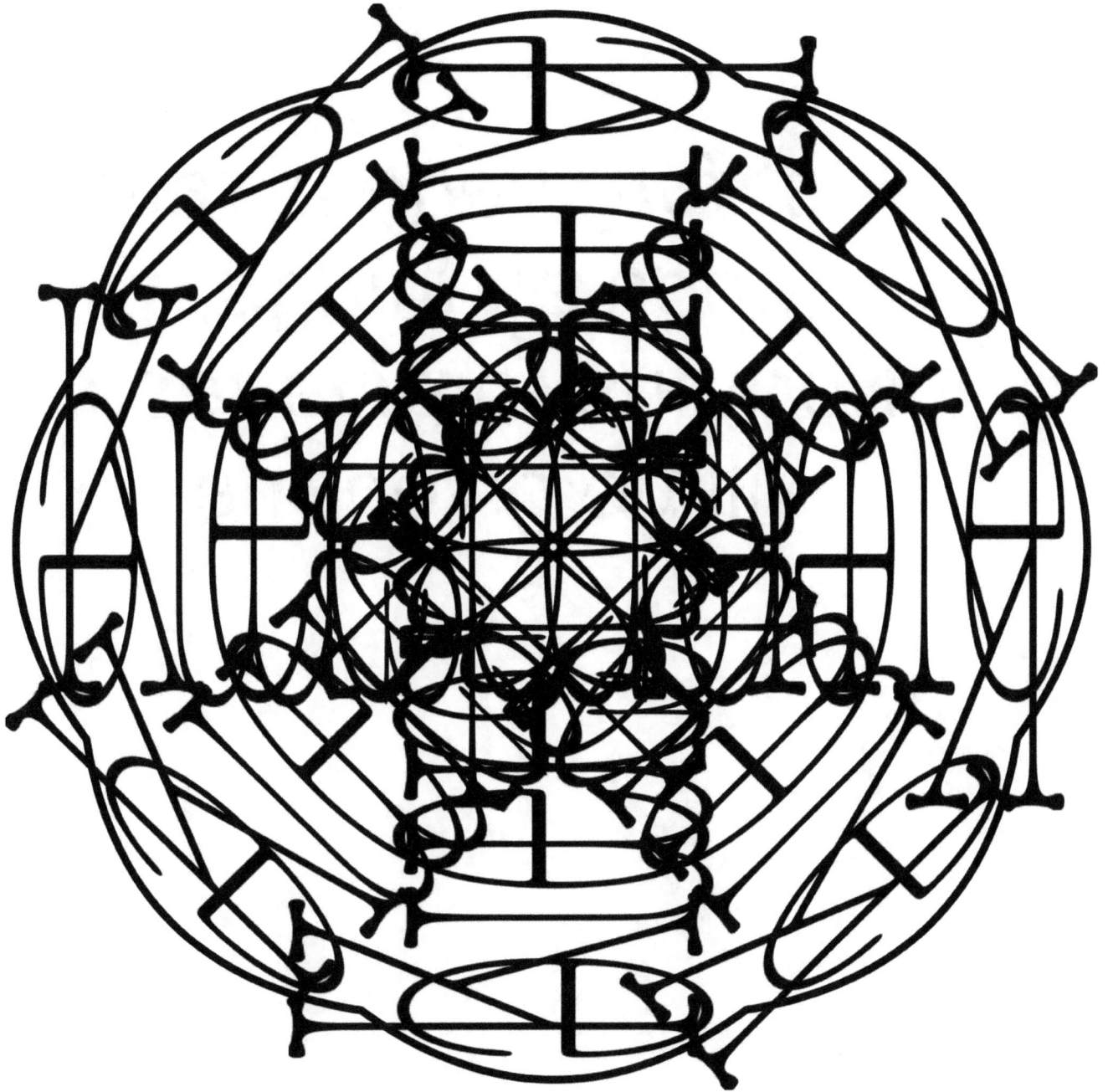

Workbook Lesson 342

I let *forgiveness* rest
upon all things,
For thus *forgiveness*
will be given me.

Forgiveness

Workbook Lesson 343

I am not asked to
make a sacrifice
To find the *mercy*
and the peace of God.

Mercy

Workbook Lesson 344

Today I learn the law
of love; that what
I give my brother
is my gift to me.

Of Love

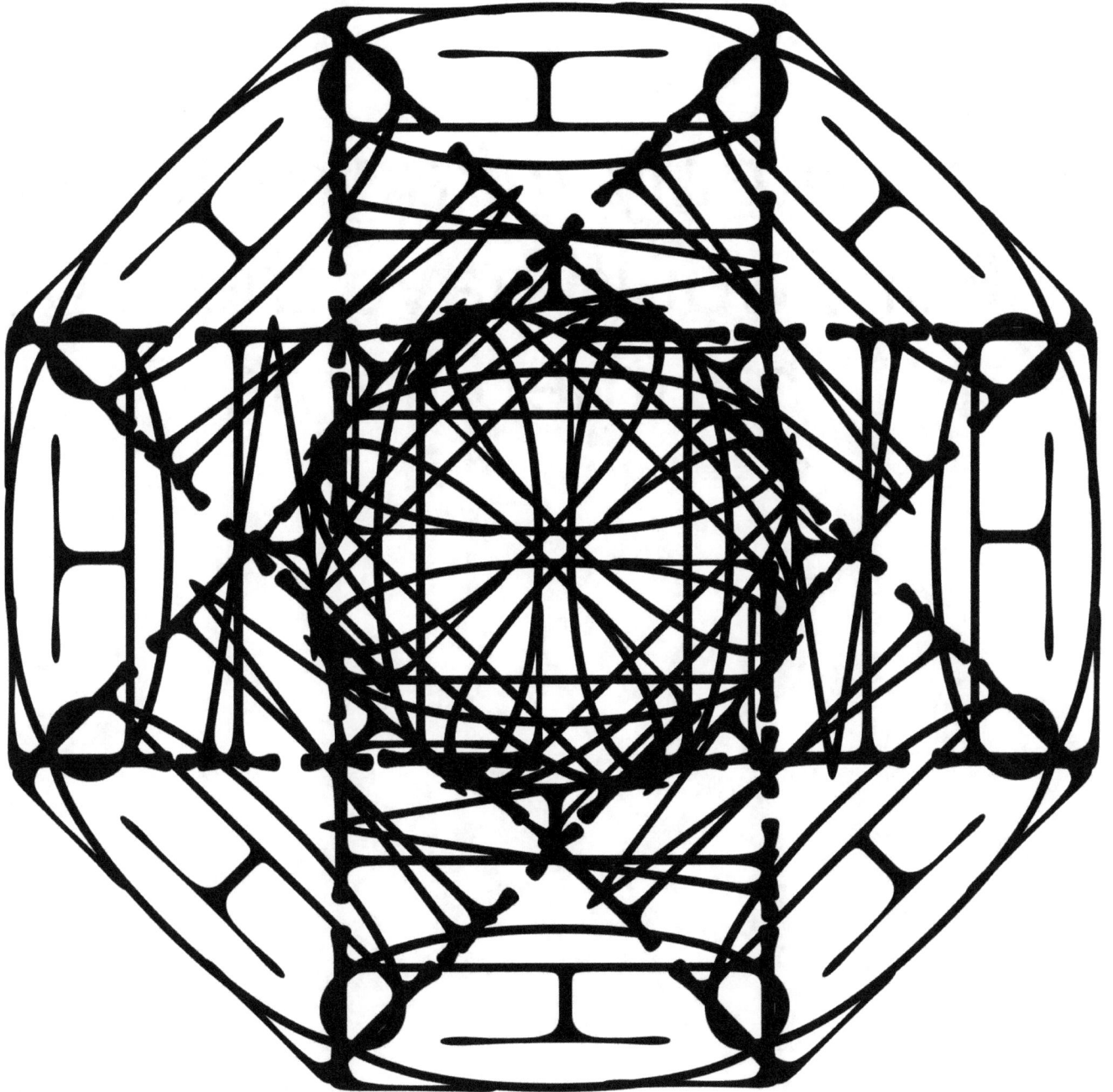

Workbook Lesson 345

I offer only *miracles* today,
For I would have them be
returned to me.

Miracles

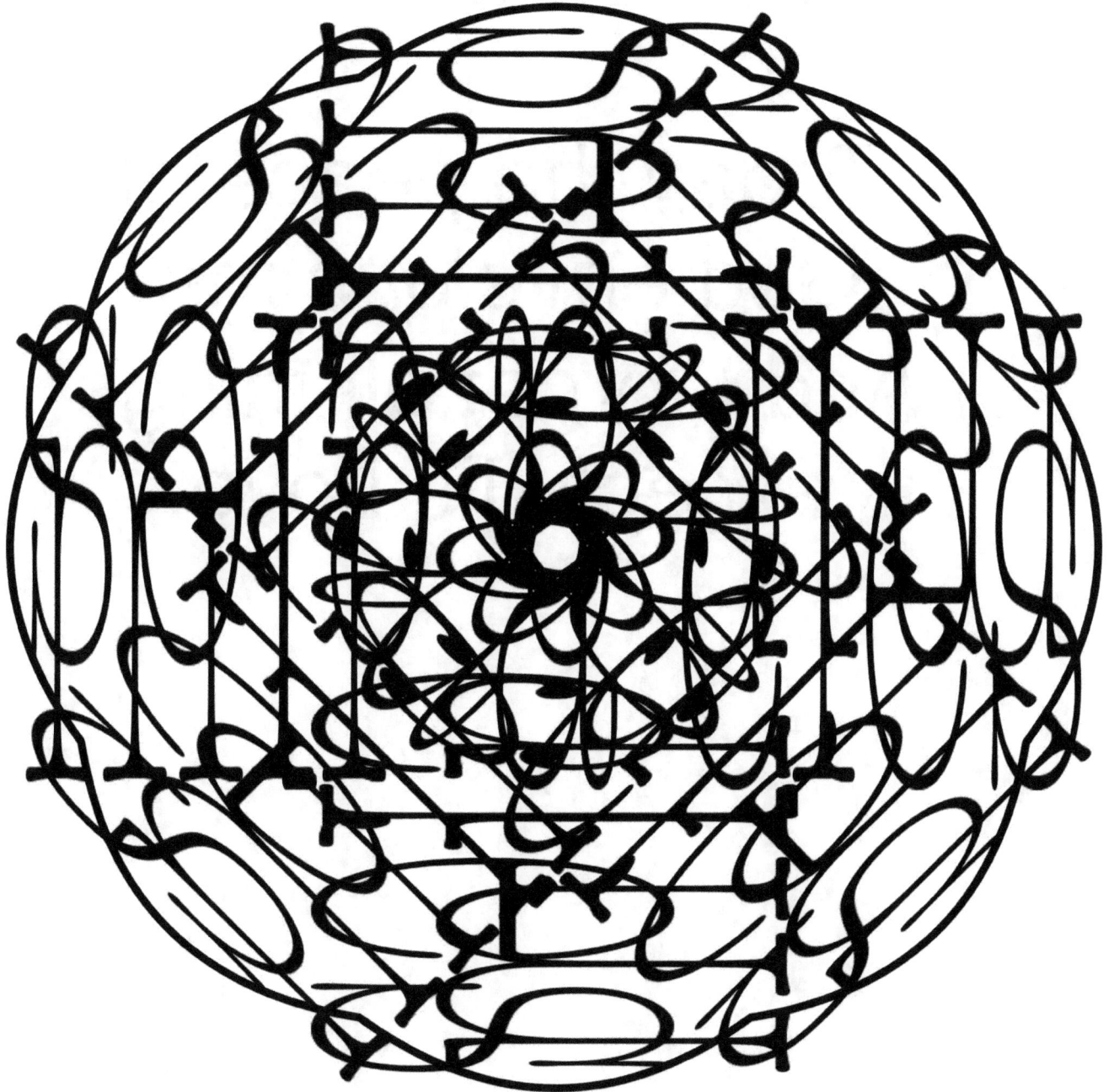

Workbook Lesson 346

Today the peace of
God *envelops* me,
And I forget all things
except His Love.

Envelops

Workbook Lesson 347

Anger must come from judgment. Judgment is The weapon I would use against myself, *To keep* the miracle away from me.

To Keep

Workbook Lesson 348

I have no cause for
anger or for fear,
For You surround me.
And in every need
That I *perceive*,
Your grace suffices me.

Perceive

Workbook Lesson 349

Today I let Christ's
vision look upon
All things for me and
judge them not, but give
Each one a miracle
of love instead.

All Things

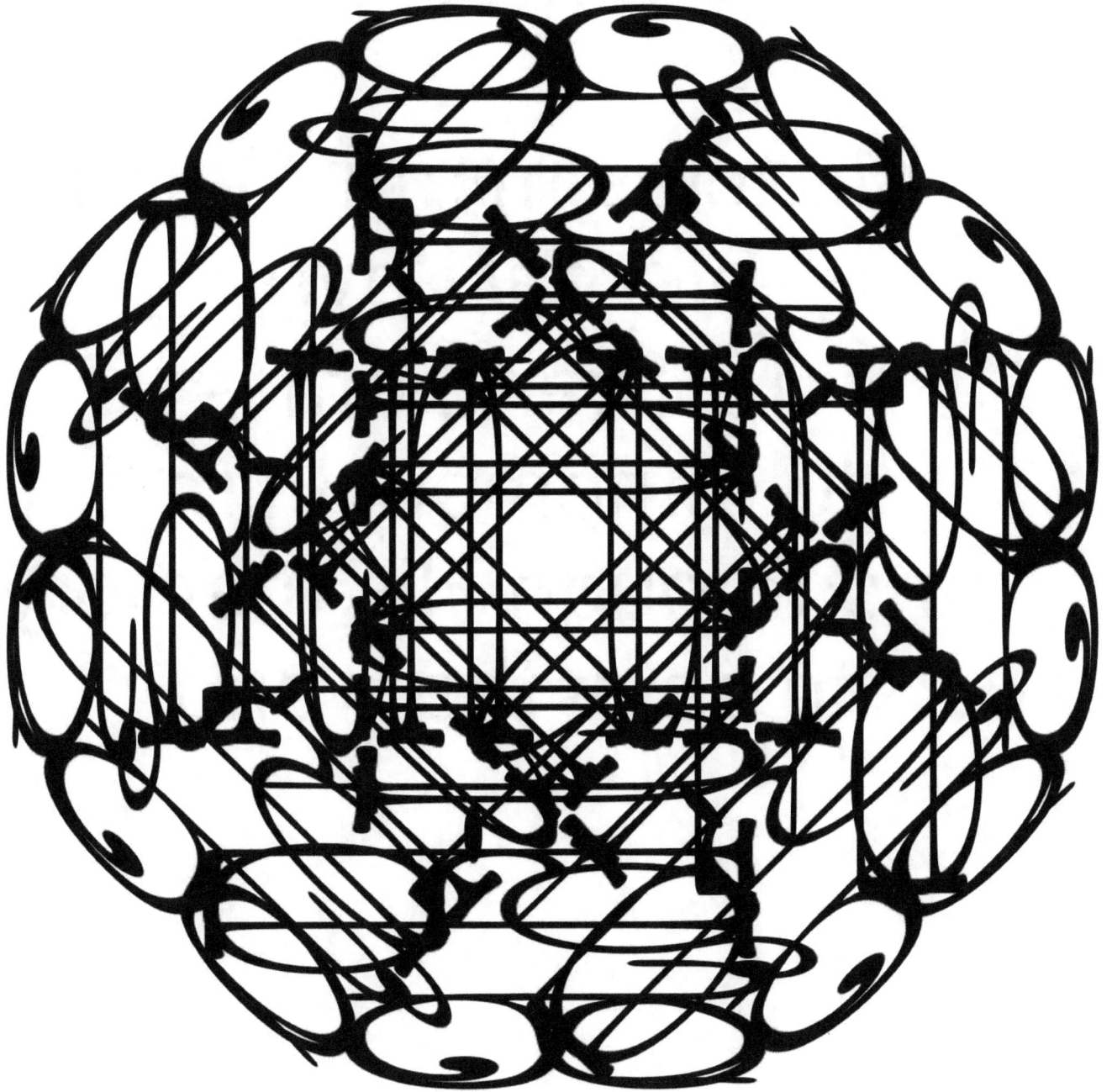

Workbook Lesson 350

Miracles mirror God's
eternal Love.
To offer them is
to remember Him,
And through His memory
to save the world.

Eternal

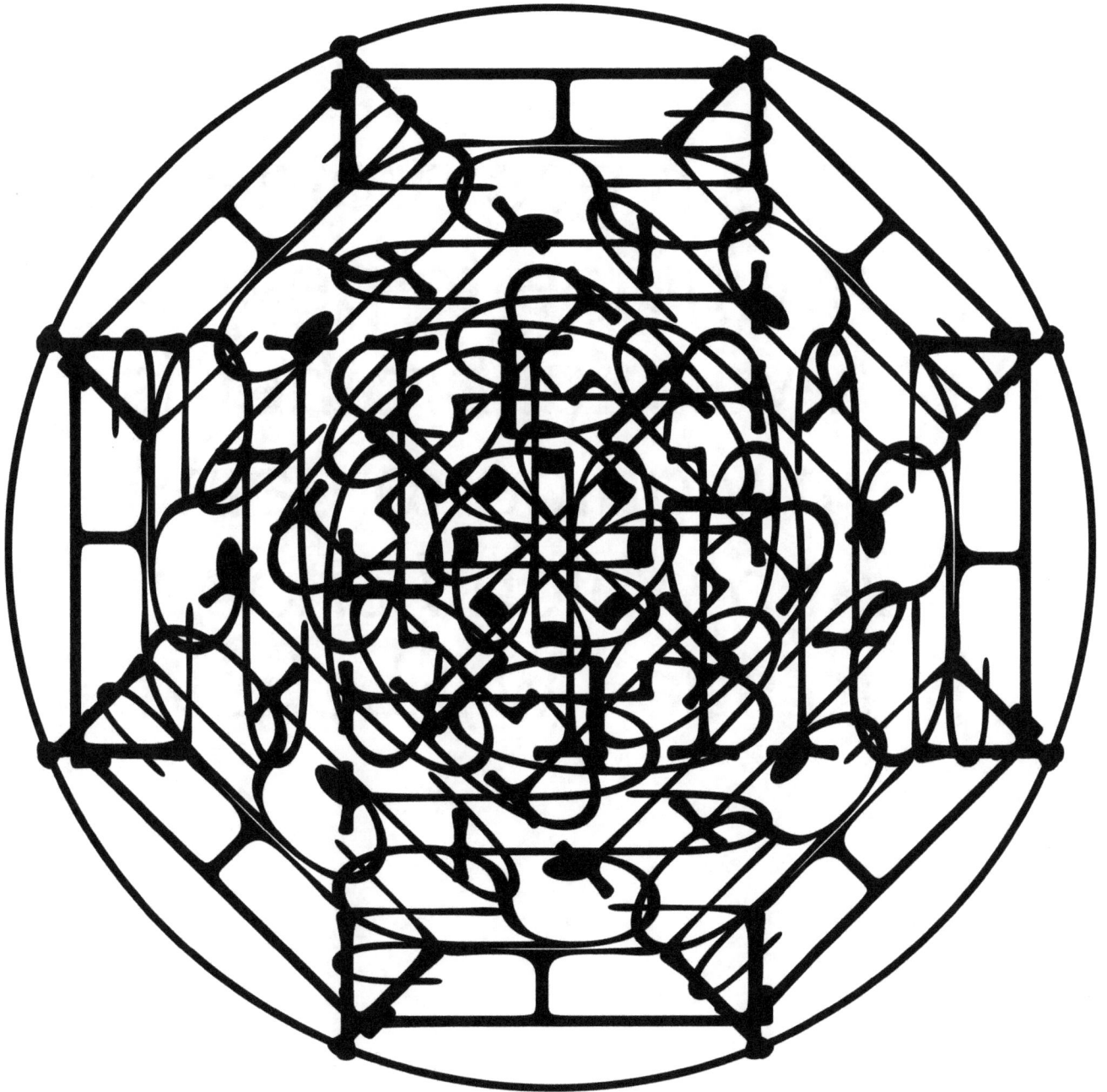

Workbook Lesson 351

My sinless brother is
my guide to peace.
My sinful brother is
my guide to pain.
And which *I choose*
to see I will behold.

I Choose

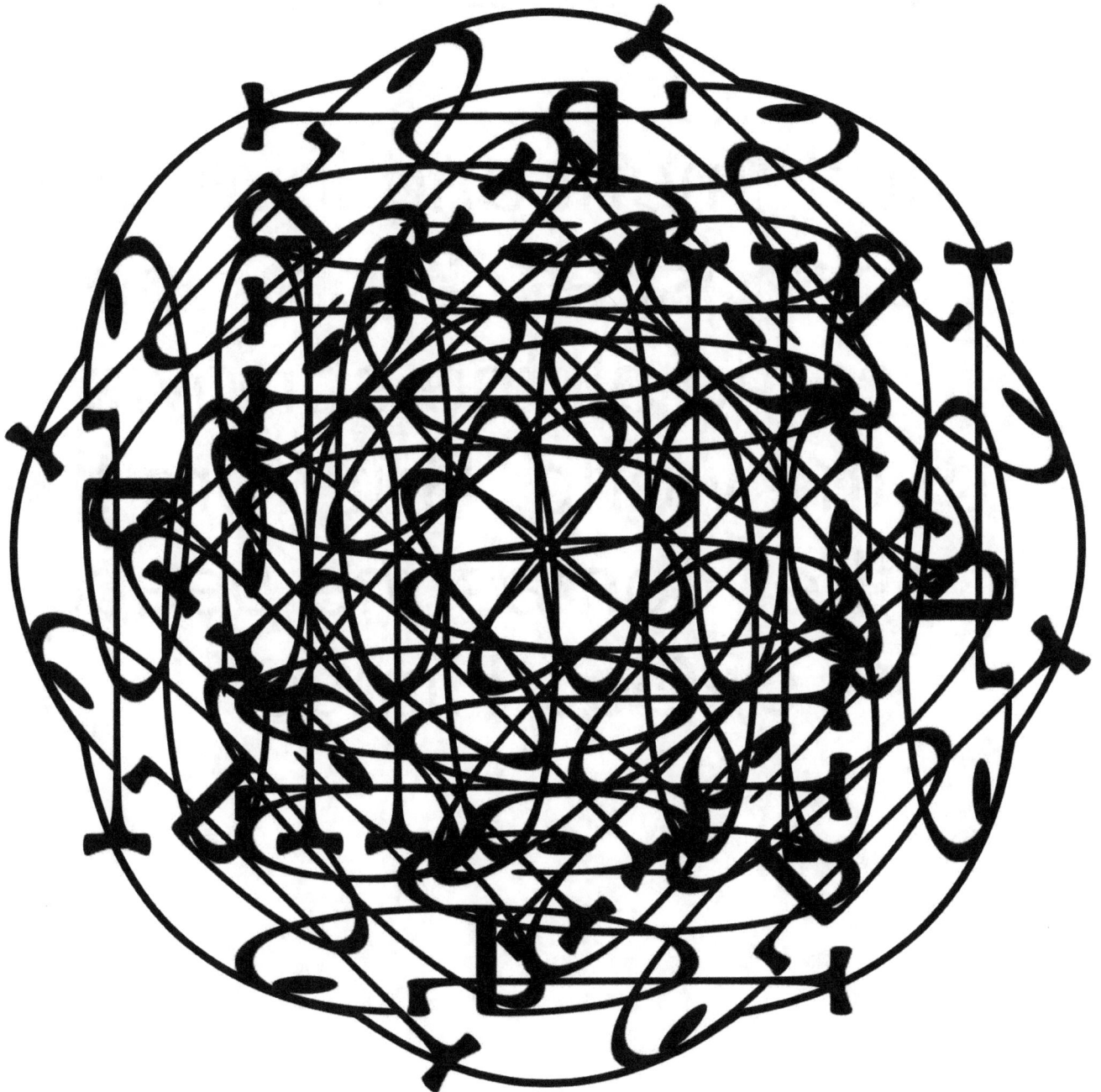

Workbook Lesson 352

Judgment and love are opposites. From one come all the sorrows of the world. But from the other comes *the peace* of God Himself.

The Peace

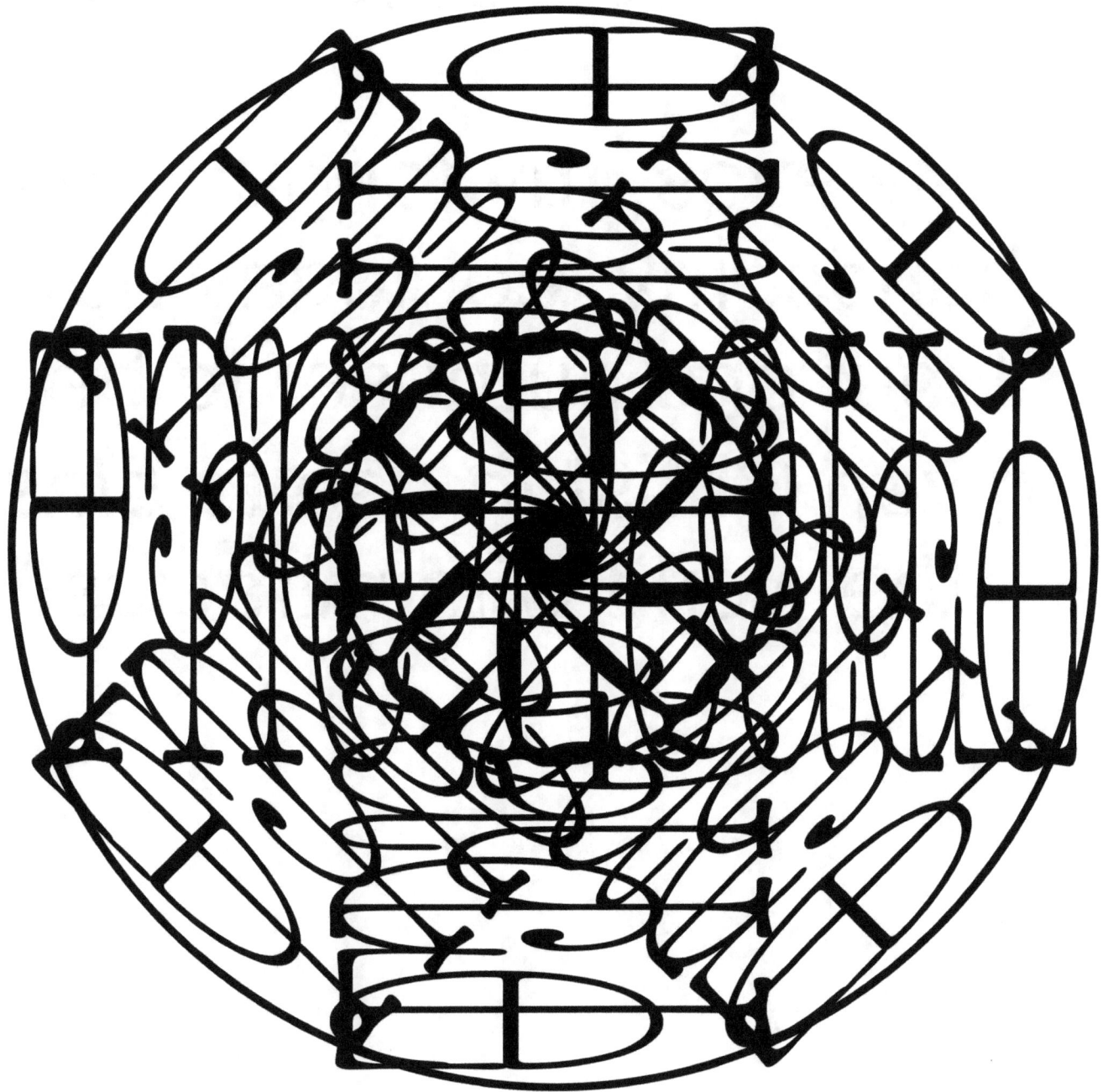

Workbook Lesson 353

My eyes, my tongue, my hands, my feet today have but one purpose; to be given Christ to use to *bless* the world with miracles.

Bless

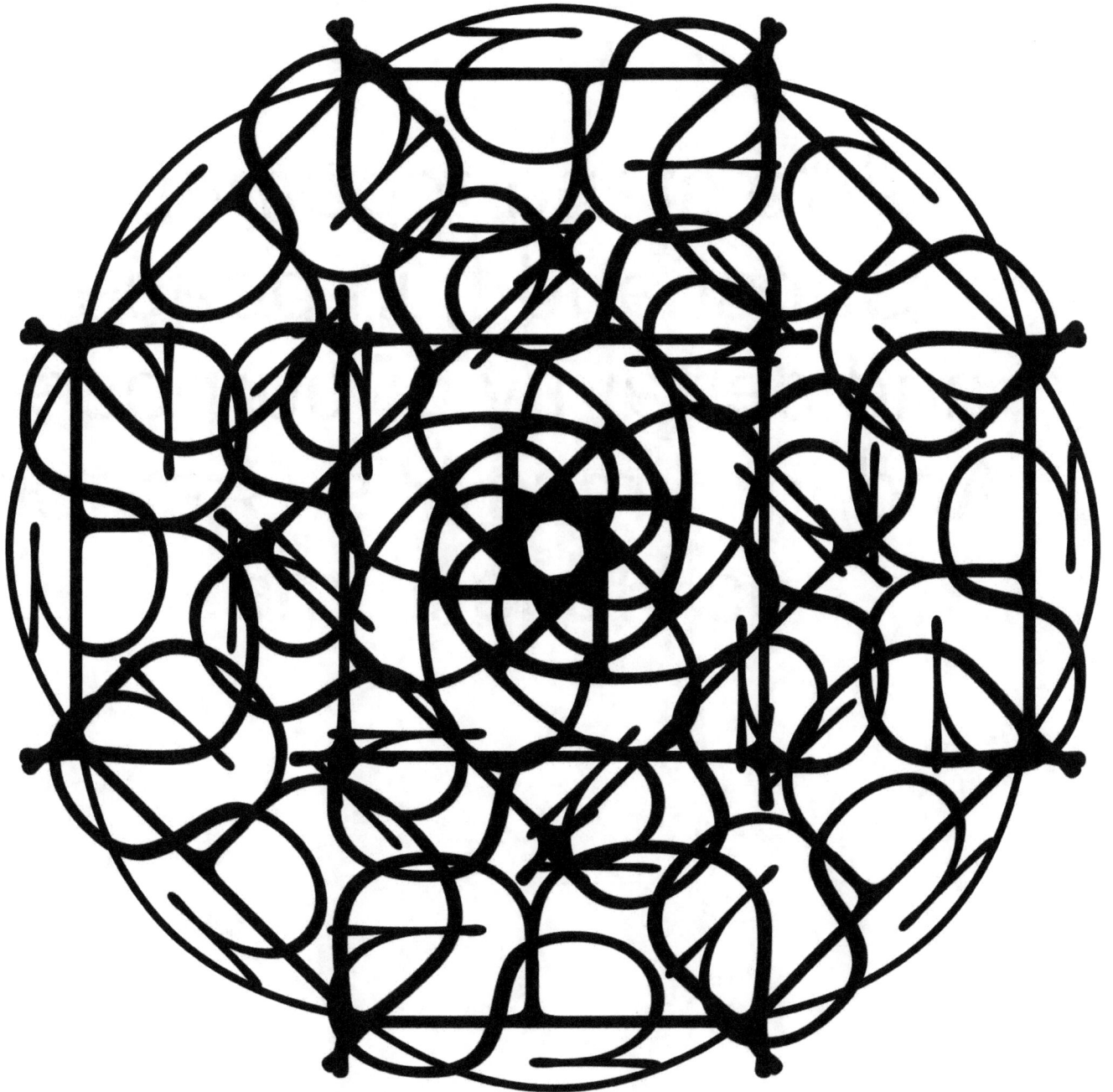

Workbook Lesson 354

We stand *together*,
Christ and I, in peace
and certainty of purpose.
And in Him is His Creator,
as He is in me.

Together

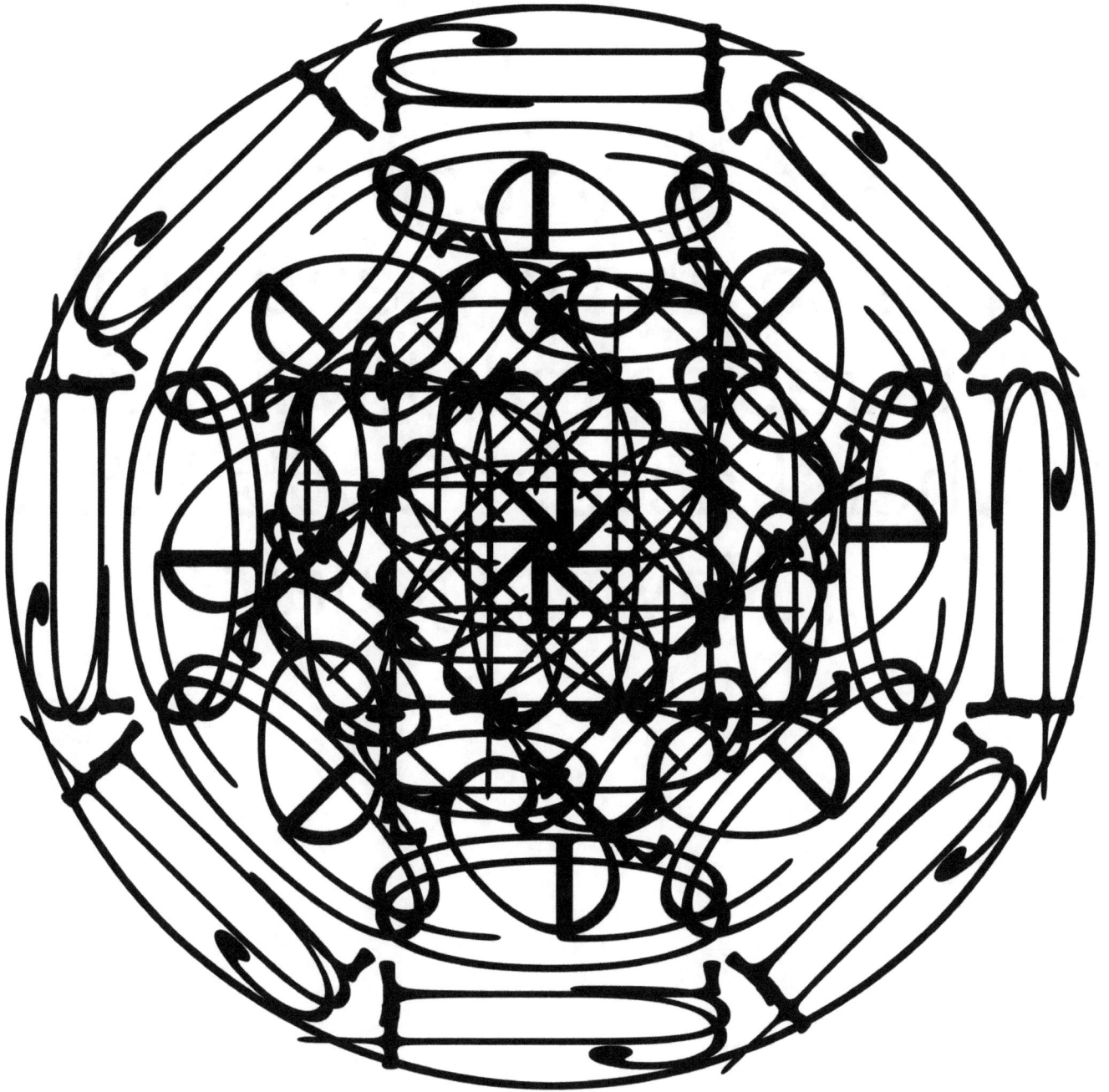

Workbook Lesson 355

There is *no end* to all the peace and joy, and all the miracles that I will give, when I accept God's Word. Why not today?

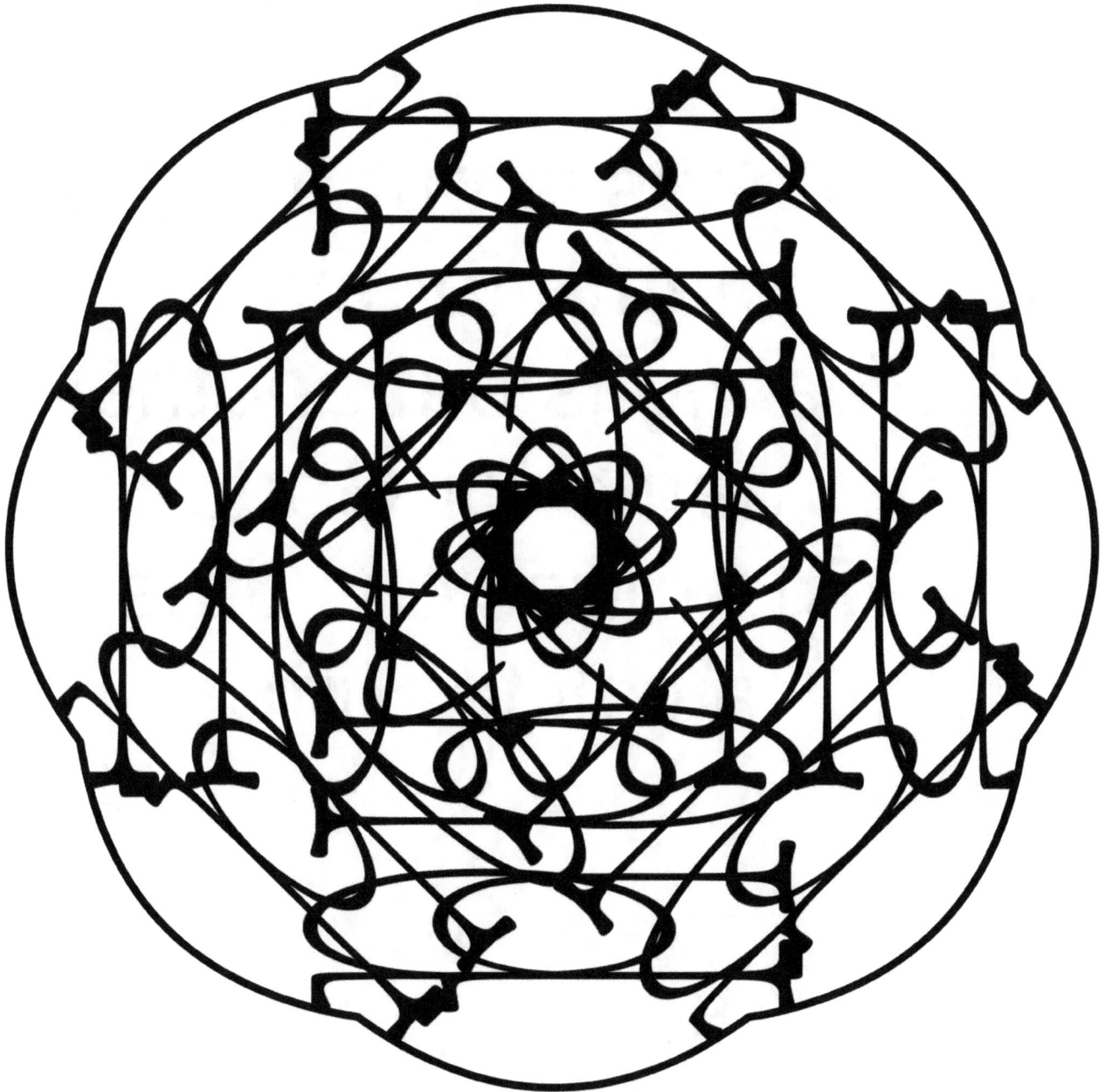

No End

Workbook Lesson 356

Sickness is but another
name for sin.
Healing is but another
name for God.
The miracle is thus
a call to Him.

Healing

Workbook Lesson 357

Truth answers every call we make to God, responding first with miracles, and then returning unto us to be itself.

Truth

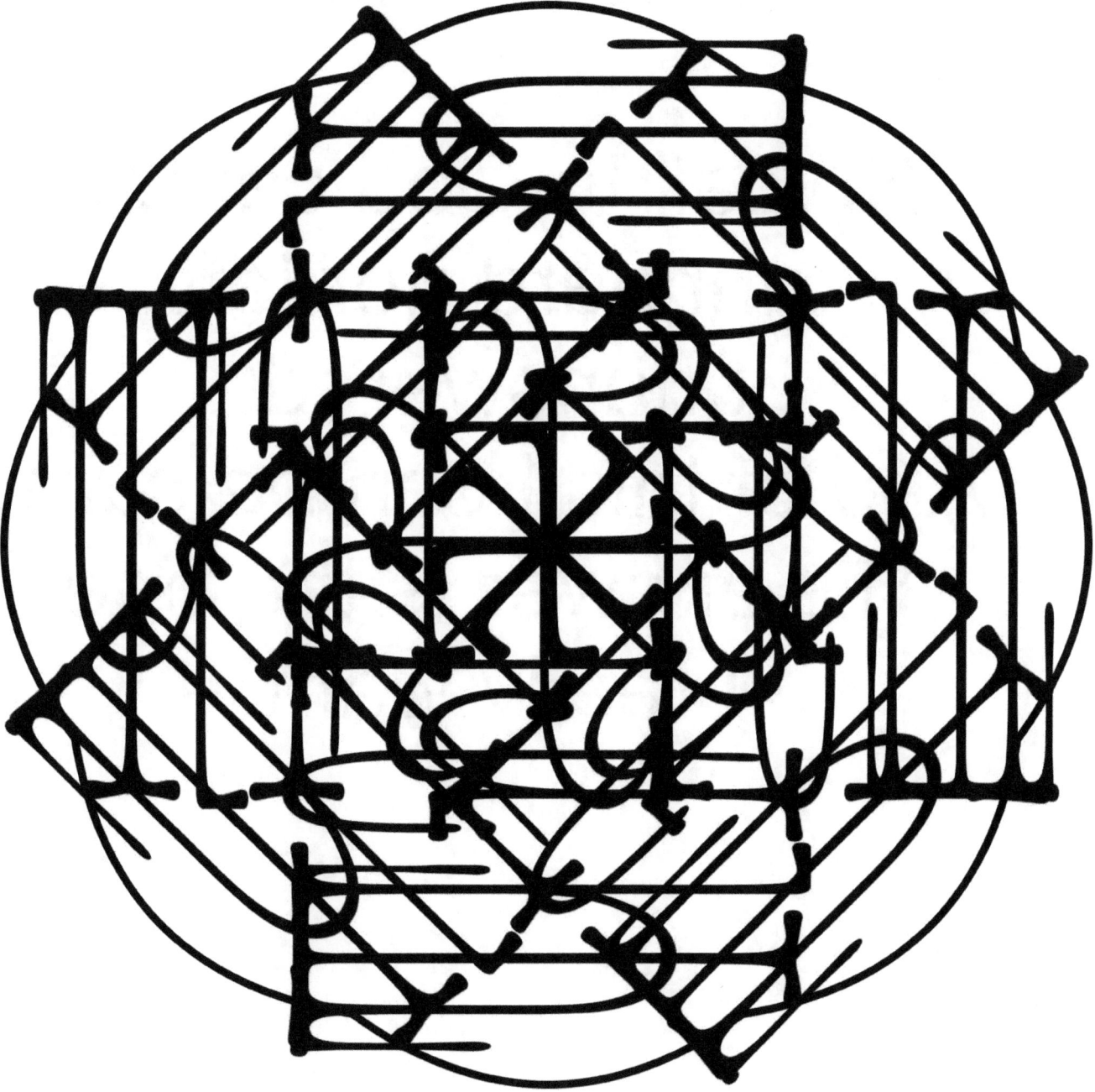

Workbook Lesson 358

No call to God can be
unheard nor left
unanswered.
And of this I can *be sure*;
His answer is the one
I really want.

Be Sure

Workbook Lesson 359

God's answer is some
form of peace. All pain is
healed; all misery
replaced *with joy*.
All prison doors
are opened. And all sin
is understood as
merely a mistake.

With Joy

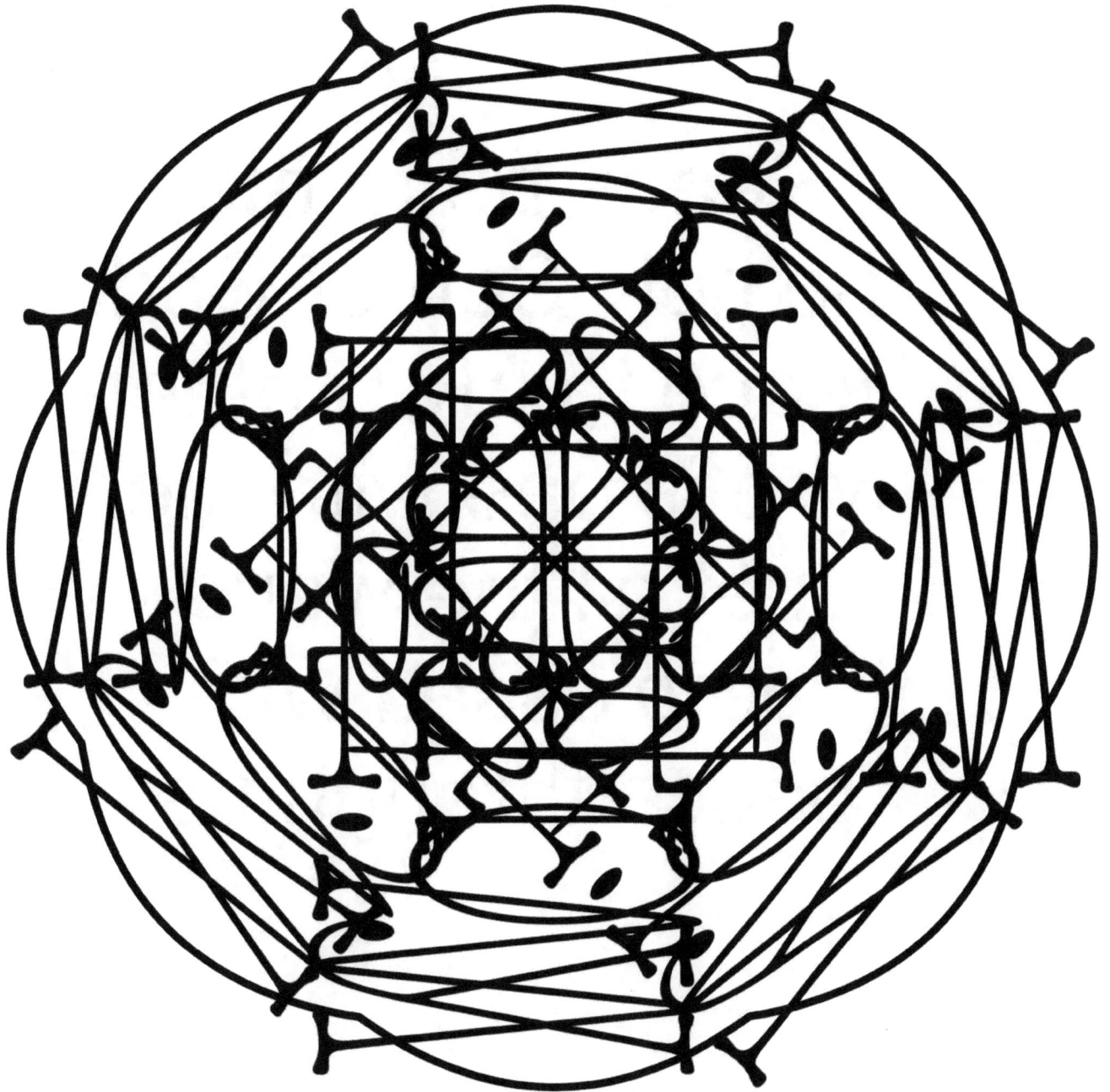

Workbook Lesson 360

Peace be to me,
the holy Son of God.
Peace to my brother,
who is one with me.
Let all the world
be *blessed* with
peace through us.

Blessed

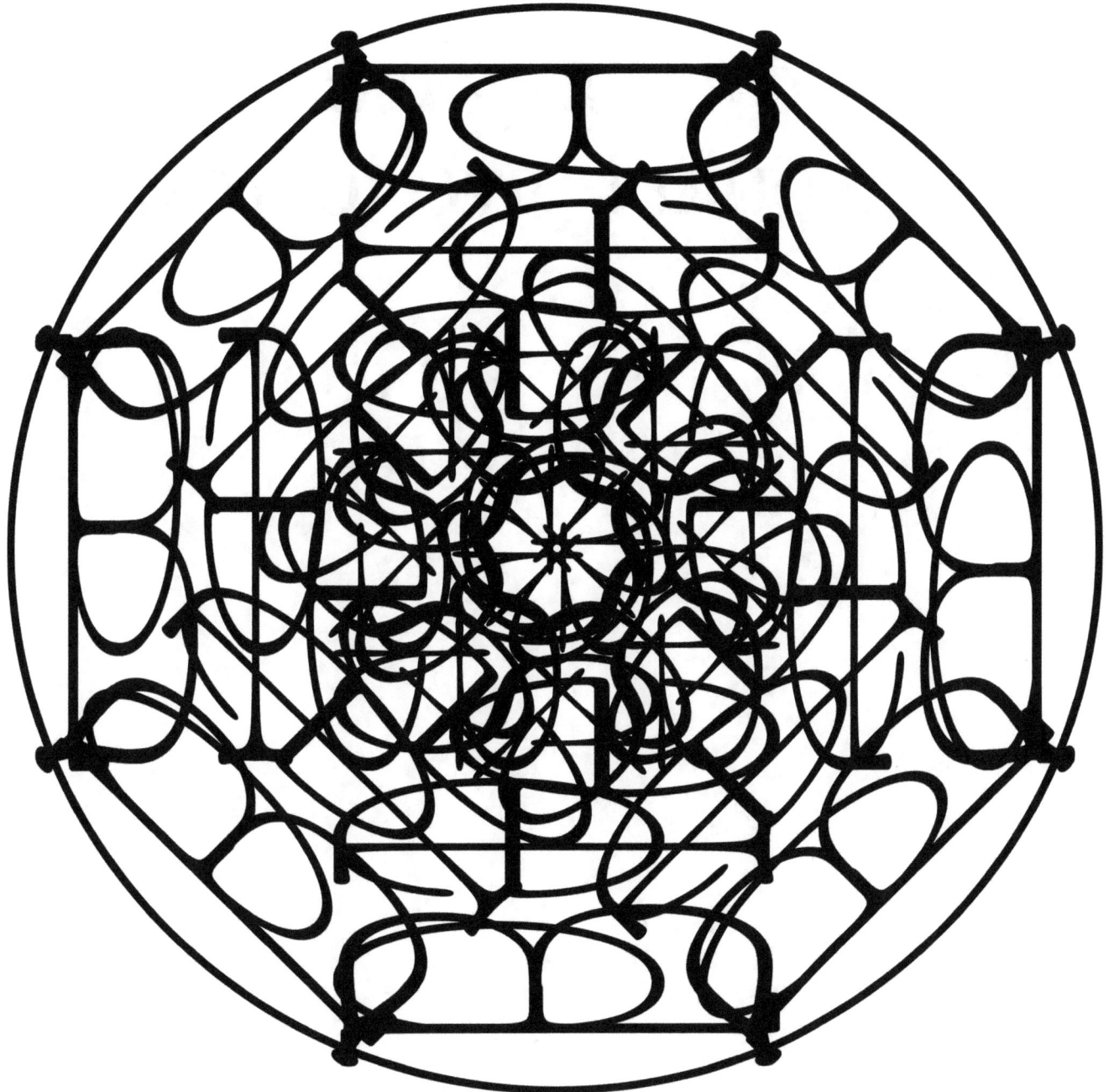

Workbook Lesson 361

This *holy instant* would I give to You.

Holy Instant

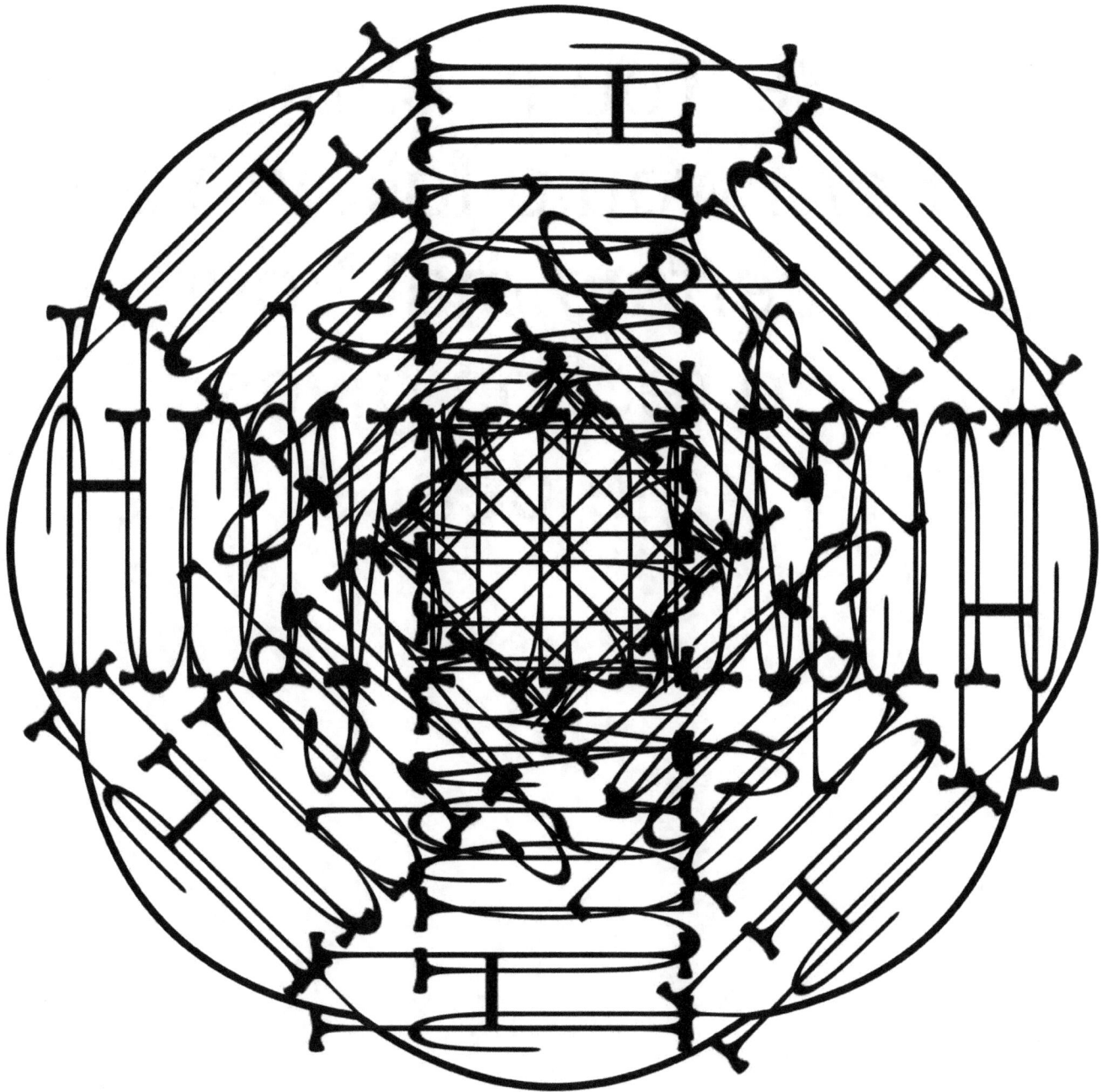

Workbook Lesson 362

Be You in charge.
For I would follow You,
certain that Your
direction gives
me peace.

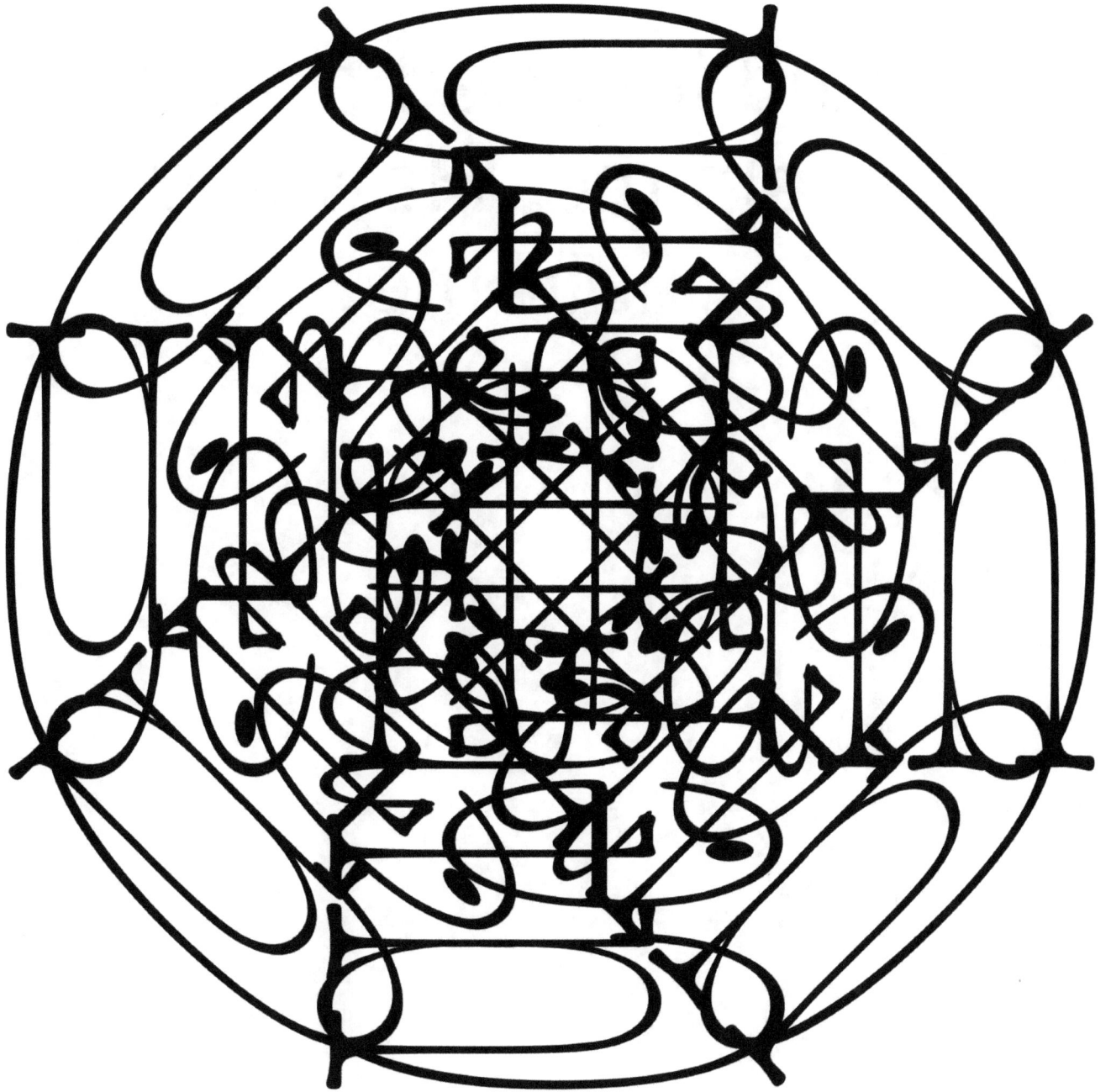

Certain

Workbook Lesson 363

And if I need *a word* to help me, He will give it to me.

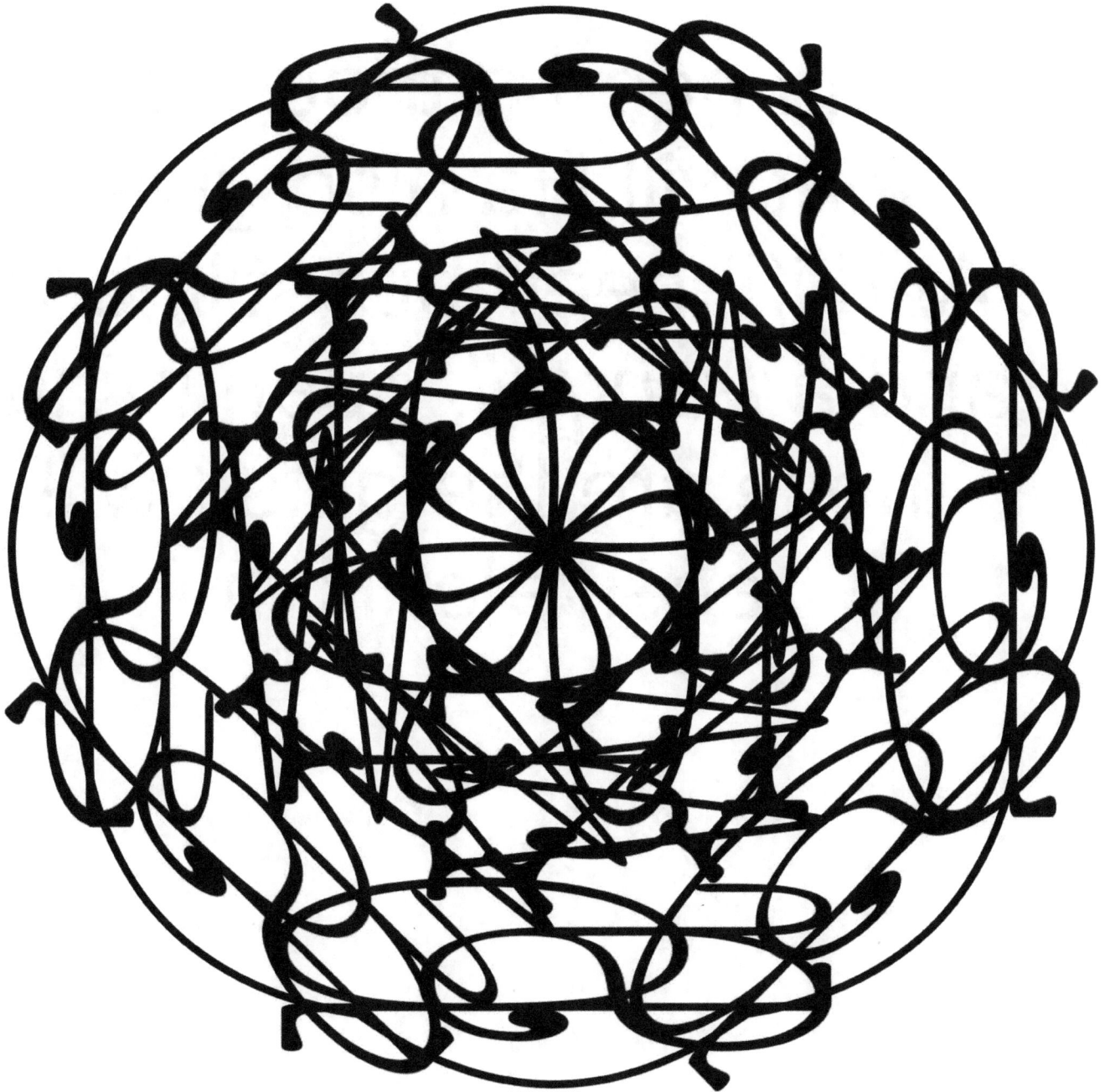

A Word

Workbook Lesson 364

If I need a thought,
that will He also give.
And if I need but stillness
and a *tranquil*, open mind,
these are the gifts I will
receive of Him.

Tranquil

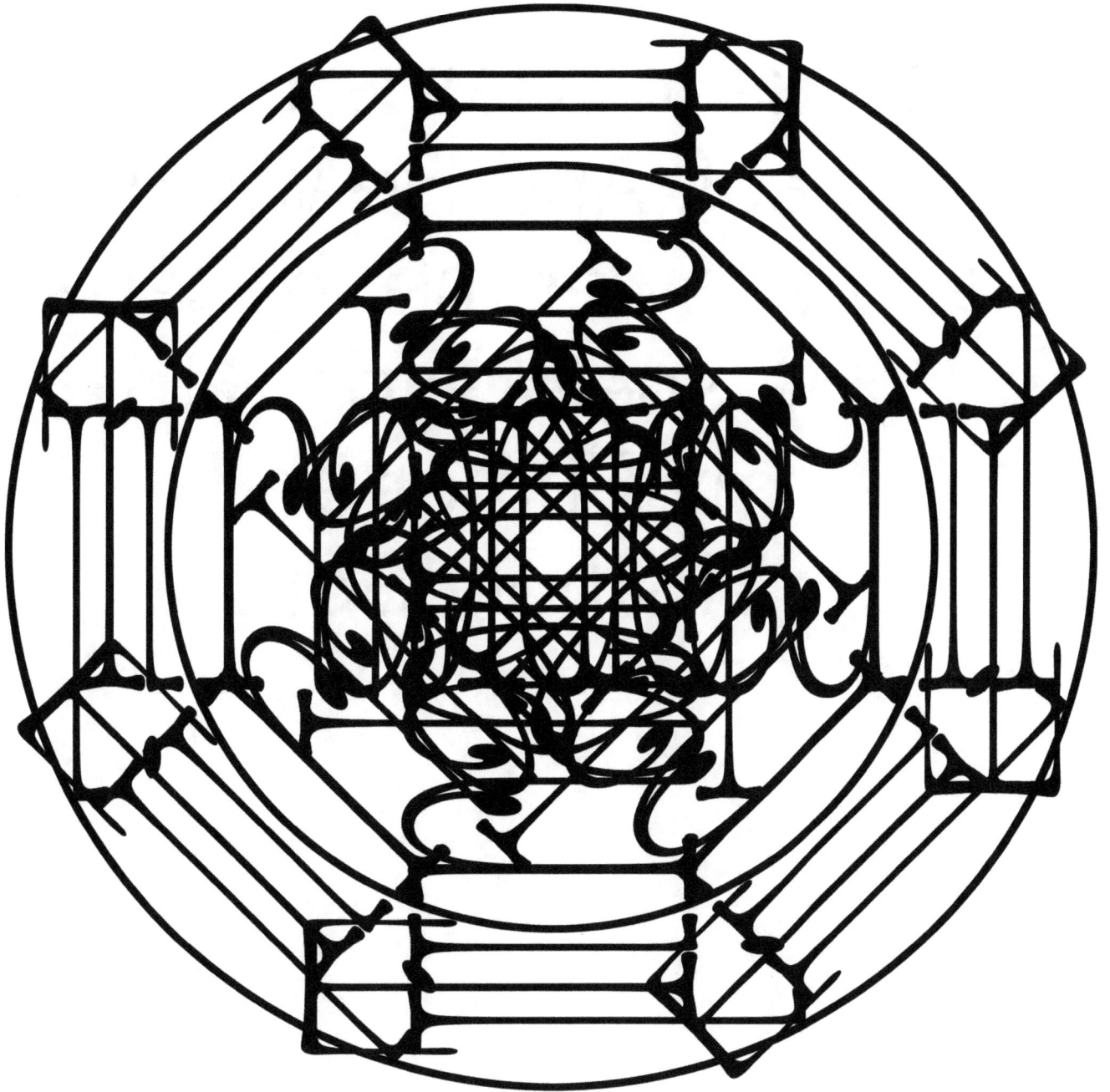

Workbook Lesson 365

He is in charge by my request. And He will hear and answer me, because He *speaks* for God my Father and His holy Son.

Speaks

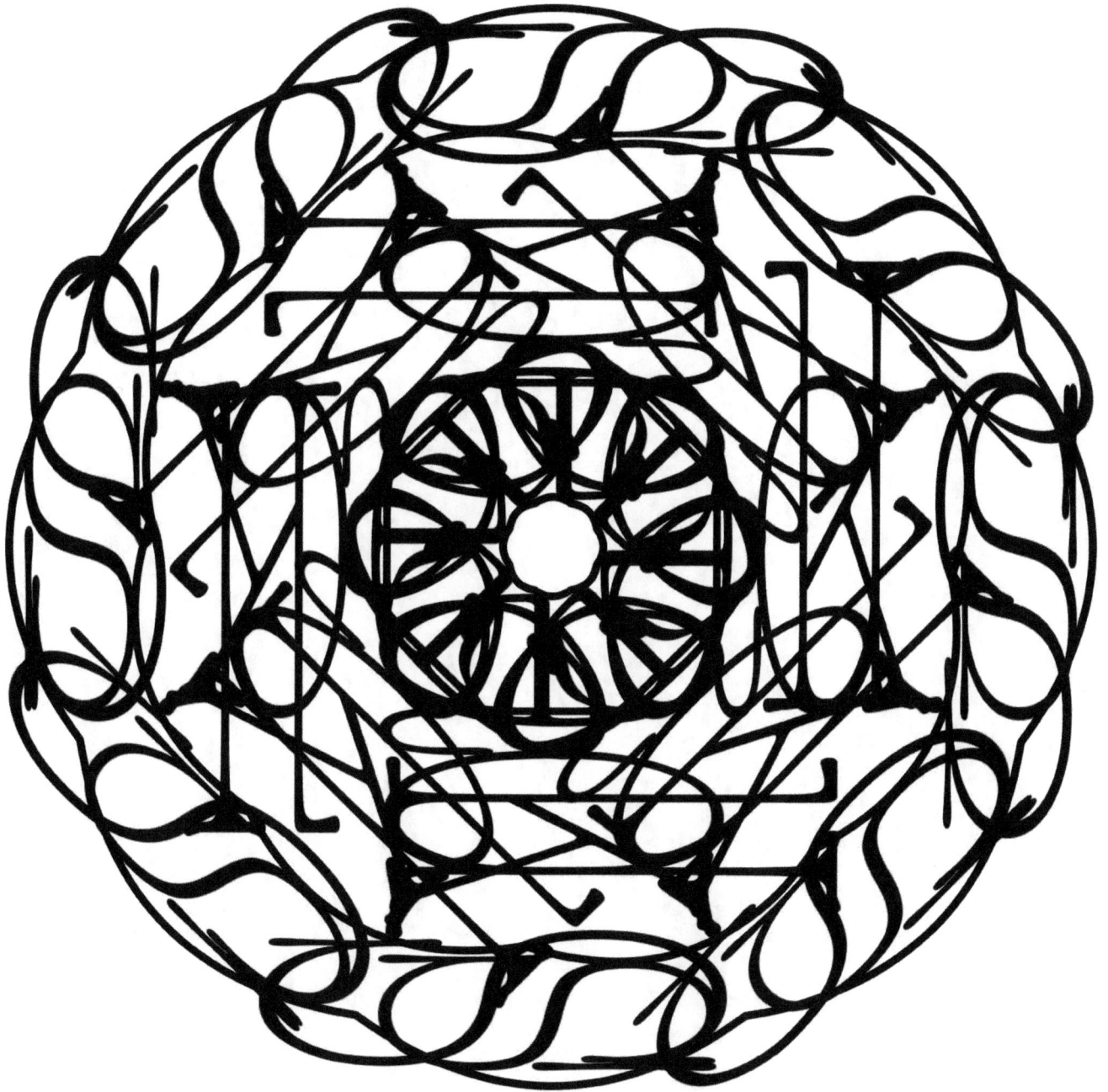

Thank you
for your purchase!

For more inspiring
Mantra Mandalas Coloring Pages™
check out:

MMColoringPages.com

Thank You!